AF472648

Ocean of Compassion

A Guide to the Life of Universal Loving

TENZIN NORBU

Cover Illustration by Eric Moore

WestBow Press books may be ordered through booksellers or by contacting:

WestBow Press
A Division of Thomas Nelson
1663 Liberty Drive
Bloomington, IN 47403
www.westbowpress.com
1-(866) 928-1240

ISBN: 978-1-4497-4092-4 (hc)
ISBN: 978-1-4497-4091-7 (sc)
ISBN: 978-1-4497-4090-0 (e)

Library of Congress Control Number: 2012902870

Printed in the United States of America

WestBow Press rev. date: 03/07/2012

Contents

I prostrate to my Spiritual Guide,
the Venerable Kelsang Gyatso, and
to all the other great philosophers
named in this book.

A precious human life,
Gateway to your final design,
Is the finest chance to progress we can have;
Don't waste this cherished time.

Introduction

Part One

Overall Scope of *Ocean of Compassion*

Shantideva (687-763 CE), by his own admission, created his masterpiece, *Guide to the Bodhisattva's Way of Life,* as an aid to his own spiritual practice. He produced a work intended to explain Mahayana Buddhist practices, which are engaged with the goal of achieving full Buddhahood for the benefit of all. Everyone can become a Buddha; all that one needs to do in order to become one is to cultivate universal, unbiased love and then engage in the practices that eventually overcome one's separation from the Ultimate Ground of All Things; however, this is more easily said than done. The purpose of this book is to aid anyone who sincerely wants to overcome his or her separation from the Ultimate Ground of All Things, which has been named using a variety words, including *God.* In Buddhism, it is called *Emptiness.* In Part III of this introduction, I will explain what the name *Emptiness* means within the context of Buddhist practice and how to understand and use the skills developed in Mahayana practice in any religion that accepts that there is an Ultimate Ground of All Things and that separation from this is the Problem of Living to be overcome. Within the monotheistic religions, I would use the name *Mystical Saint* to talk about what Buddhists call a Buddha. A mystical saint is someone who is motivated by universal, unbiased love and who has overcome separation from God.

I imagine that the verses Shantideva wrote served as starting points for analytical meditation as well as guideposts for his thoughts, words, and actions. I will explain what I mean by analytical meditation in Parts II and III of this introduction. Although I may or may not be correct about the purposes Shantideva undertook when he wrote *Guide to the Bodhisattva's Way of Life,* these are definitely the purposes for which I have written my verses. Although I have long depended upon the inspiration I have drawn from Shantideva's verses, I have found that the verses themselves—at least in their English translations, and to which in this form alone I have access—do not engage my imagination fully. My own failure in imagination—not the power of Shantideva's messages themselves—has led to my writing the verses in this work, *Ocean of Compassion, A Guide to the Life of Universal Loving.* I have found that the power the message has to engage my imagination is enhanced by presenting the message in relatively simple ways in rhyming verse. Using one of more verses related to the development of a particular attainment in an internal, repetitious recitation during a meditation session can help to induce the emotive reactions and intellectual conclusions sought in Mahayana meditation. Many of these verses, therefore, have become my personal mantras both for the pursuit of meditational goals as well as to protect my mind from negative thoughts and emotions. The verses have served to alter my thoughts, words, and behavior in positive ways.

Bodhichitta, the intention to become a Buddha for the benefit of all sentient beings, is the "pure, superior intention," the adoption of which allows one to pass through the gateway to the Mahayana and become a Son or Daughter of the Buddha—a Bodhisattva. You will become a Bodhisattva when this intention becomes the ultimate purpose of your life. It does not matter by what name you are then called—it may be Bodhisattva, it may be Christ-like Lover, or it may be any other name that is suitable. What is important is that at this point, you will sincerely strive with all of your efforts to subsume every one of your actions under this goal. That is to say, you will endeavor to make the particular objective of each of your thoughts, words, and actions a means to reach your final objective of becoming a Buddha for the benefit of all.

A Buddha/Mystical Saint has the maximum capability possible to guide sentient beings to the ultimate happiness of union with the Ultimate Ground of All Things. Buddhas and Mystical Saints can do this because they have done it, so they know the correct spiritual path to follow. In our ignorance, we constantly act in ways that frustrate our desire to achieve lasting happiness, and our actions continually throw us into uncontrolled rebirths in which we experience frustration and suffering. Until we are able to overcome our ignorance, we experience this repetitive cycle of frustration. What we ordinarily seek and get, at best, brings us temporary relief from frustration or results in a transitory feeling we identify as pleasure.

Tragically, the transitory feelings we think are true pleasures often become our obsessions, and we lust after them as if experiencing them over and over again constitutes true and lasting happiness. In fact, these obsessions blind us to what does bring true and lasting happiness, and so they prevent us from acting in ways that will actually bring this to us. That there is a mode of being in which true and lasting happiness is experienced and that everyone can reach this mode of being are among the articles of faith of Bodhisattvas. Until one becomes a Buddha, one needs this faith, but it is far from a blind faith, as there have been countless models—both contemporary and stretching back to the time of Shakyamuni Buddha—of those who have achieved this mode of being. Everyone wants lasting happiness; each of us should hope that everyone can experience lasting happiness, and it is possible for everyone to reach a mode of being in which true and lasting happiness is experienced. As a Bodhisattva, you will embark on the path that ends when you attain the mode of being in which you can help every sentient being reach this goal. How could any purpose of action have any real, objective worth whatsoever if it is not useful as a means to help everyone achieve lasting and true happiness?

You cannot become a Buddha/Mystical Saint unless you want to be one, as is true with just about any important goal, be it a mundane, worldly goal or supra mundane, spiritual goal. Choosing Buddhahood as your destination is known as having "aspiring Bodhichitta." It is not possible to stumble into Buddhahood; you have to know this is where you want to go in order to get to this destination. Moreover, it is not possible to get to this destination unless you actually go down the correct spiritual path by your own efforts. As a hitchhiker, you might choose Chicago as your destination and actually be able to get there, but you cannot hitchhike to Buddhahood. No one else can drive you down this path; others can only point out the way. It is up to you to drive the great vehicle (the "Mahayana") to Buddhahood. Actually taking the steps toward this goal is known as "engaging Bodhichitta." The first chapter, "Cultivating Bodhichitta," contains my reflections on the tried and true methods for cultivating both aspiring and engaging Bodhichitta. The ideas and techniques presented in these verses are drawn from Shantideva and other sages with vastly more knowledge and experience than I have. However, these verses have proven useful to me, and they may be useful to you.

Having cultivated both aspiring and rudimentary, engaging Bodhichitta, one has the motivation and disposition necessary to travel the whole path. At this point, one needs the map that shows the way, and one must attempt to understand and follow the map. The directions about what are the thoughts, words, and actions of someone walking the path are contained in the time-proven teachings on the six perfections: Generosity, Patience, Moral Discipline, Effort, Concentration, and Wisdom. Chapters 2 through 7 contain verses expressing my understandings of the thoughts, words, and actions that constitute the expression of these six perfections. Anything at all that is true or useful in these verses comes from the teachings of my Spiritual Guide and the sage words of other past masters. I have tried to understand and follow the teachings, and I am passing along what I have learned in my own words hoping that my way of explaining the path will be helpful to others.

The six perfections are frequently enumerated in the order given in the previous paragraph. They are not, however, practiced serially, as if one first masters Generosity and then moves on to the others in succession. They are all pursued concurrently, with each chosen behavior at any particular time being that which is most appropriate given the current situation. Perhaps at a particular time, all things considered, one should behave patiently rather than behaving generously if one does not, at that time, have the ability to express both perfections simultaneously. Perhaps in preventing anger, one does not have the mental resources available for wishing and praying that sentient beings not suffer from natural disasters. On the other hand, in generating Patience toward someone who might otherwise become the object of your anger, you might at the same time be Generous in bringing to mind that you are being Patient toward him or her so as to become a Buddha in order to lead everyone—including him or her—to Buddhahood. Your behavior in this case would simultaneously express both Patience and Generosity. Effort must accompany all of the other perfections, and for this reason, I have chosen to present my reflections on the engaging Bodhichitta of Effort first among the perfections as Chapter 2. If one cultivates Effort—the mode of thinking and feeling in which one rejoices in and experiences pleasure from one's own and others' virtuous thoughts, words, and deeds—all of the other perfections naturally begin to evolve.

In the same way that Effort can be thought to have priority of place because of its laying the groundwork for the development of all the other perfections, Wisdom is last in place of development, because this perfection cannot be brought to full fruition unless the mind can rest in Concentration upon a very subtle intellectual object of understanding—the true nature of all phenomena. Ordinarily, our minds are very distracted and move from object to object in a disorganized manner. This lack of focus and disorganization is caused by the mental garbage that has accumulated within our minds from our past non-virtuous actions. Because of this, we cannot maintain focus on a single object of thought for more than a few fleeting moments. In order to discern the subtle nature of all phenomena, which constitutes Wisdom, we must have a concentrated, non-distracted mind, and we cannot develop this kind of mind until we rid our mind of its haphazard, distracted manner of operation. In order to do this, we must first rid our minds of vicious thoughts, words, and deeds through Moral Discipline. Then we can successfully employ the methods for developing Concentration. For this reason, my reflections on the perfection of Wisdom conclude the book as Chapter 7, my reflections on Concentration are presented in Chapter 6, and my reflections on the perfection of Moral Discipline are presented in Chapter 5. Upon mastering Wisdom, you will have achieved the final goal—Buddhahood/Mystical Sainthood.

When I began to write these verses, the purpose I had in mind was to assist myself and other Buddhists in practicing Mahayana Buddhism. However, the underlying theme of Mahayana practice—love and compassion for all—is a theme universally shared as of central importance in all of the major religions currently practiced. In monotheistic religions, God is Love, and this implies not only that God should be venerated for this, but humans should strive, in so far as possible, to become more godly by becoming more loving and compassionate. Buddhism teaches that we should not classify sentient beings into friends, enemies, and strangers. Rather we should regard everyone as a being to be loved. As previously mentioned, we are called a Son or Daughter of the Buddha when we have love for all and strive to acquire the capacity to actually help everyone. By way of comparison, Jesus said, "You have heard the law that says, 'Love your neighbor and hate your enemy.' But I say, love your enemies! Pray for those who persecute you! In that way, you will be acting as true children of your Father in heaven. For He gives His sunlight to both the evil and the good, and He sends rain on the just and the unjust alike." (Matthew: 43-46) The Koran gives the following guidance: "And what will explain to you what the steep path is? It is the freeing of a (slave) from bondage; or the giving of food in a day of famine to an orphan relative, or to a needy in distress. Then will he be of those who believe, enjoin fortitude and encourage kindness and compassion." (90:12-17) Judaism also teaches this universal love: "Do not take revenge, do not bear a grudge against a member of your people, love thy neighbor like thyself." (Vayikra, Parshas Kedoshim, 19: 18)

All monotheistic religions urge humans to become more Godly not only in following God's law, but also by developing into more loving and compassionate persons. Furthermore, the perfections of Generosity, Patience, Moral Discipline, and Effort are also of universal importance. Concentration and Wisdom are the capstone perfections, because anyone can use them to attain a mystical union with the Ultimate Ground of All Things, God. I hope that much of what is found in the verses of this book can be helpful to anyone, no matter what his or her religious background may be. One could easily exchange "Bodhichitta" with "Godly loving" or "Christ-like loving," and the verses on the praise and development of Bodhichitta could then be as useful to monotheists as to Buddhists. If this would be helpful to you in the pursuit of your spiritual goals, then you may feel free to substitute one name for another. Ultimately, these are only names, and when we engage in naming, we are turning something which is dynamic into something that is static. When we make static things with our minds, we can't do anything important with them.

Compare the following verses in this work concerning the development of Effort and Generosity with Matthew 6:19-21. Both use words to try to do something dynamic that will advance our development, and the dynamic change sought is similar, though it is expressed in different ways of looking at "things."

From Chapter 2:

Please know another form of sloth:
The Attractions we must skirt.
Meaningless and non-virtuous acts
Are the doings to avert.

These worldly enjoyments are like a flame,
And we are like a moth.
The wheel of woe tightly entraps us, as we
Fly toward the holocaust.

From Chapter 3:

One of the tangible things we can give
Is an admired article we own.
Grasping the palpable goods we possess
Cannot bring happiness; this is well-known.

Every tangible item we buy
Will eventually disappear.
So, how can clenching things ephemeral
Bring us that which is lasting and dear?

"Do not store up for yourselves treasures on earth, where moth and rust consume and where thieves break in and steal; but store up for yourselves treasures in heaven, where neither moth nor rust consumes and where thieves do not break in and steal. For where your treasure is, there your heart will be also" (Matthew 6:19-21).

I share the belief of His Holiness, the Dalai Lama, that the members of different religious traditions can develop an appreciation for religious diversity while at the same time remaining true to their own traditions. In April of 2008, he said, "As you know, I always believed, since all different traditions have the same potential to bring inner peace, inner value . . . it is important to keep one's own tradition." Because we all share an appreciation for the values of inner peace and the expression of loving kindness through virtues such as generosity and patience, we all have a common heritage. Let us express our common values through meaningful thoughts, words, and deeds that benefit all.

A Note on Parts II and III of the Introduction

Chapters 6 and 7 are primarily for those who want to end all suffering through the skills attained as a result of achieving union with the Ultimate Ground of All Things out of the motive of love for all sentient beings. In Buddhism, the Ultimate Ground of All Things is called *Emptiness* or *interdependent co-origination.* The word *Emptiness* means there is nothing which exists as a thing-separate, i.e. all things are empty of self-existence. In monotheism, the Ultimate Ground of All Things it is called God. Chapter 7 contains very complicated philosophical arguments which must be understood in order to achieve union with the Ultimate Ground of All Things. Although Chapter 7 contains sophisticated arguments, it is quite likely that most people will find it very interesting to read, even if the reader doesn't completely understand the arguments. Various funny things happen to a character named Ella in this chapter, and the book comes to a dramatic conclusion expressed in emotionally moving metaphors. For those who would prefer to wait for a discussion of the philosophical arguments until later, it is best to skip reading Parts II and III of this Introduction and just begin reading Chapter 1 now. Parts II and III of the introduction explain the purpose of Chapter 6 and the philosophical arguments of Chapter 7.

Part II

Chapter 6 of *Ocean of Compassion*

Chapter 6 defines nine levels of ability to bring the mind to rest on a mental content of consciousness, and it explains how to recognize when you have developed a particular level. For those who want to try to develop these levels, it may be necessary to find a deeper explanation of these and how to achieve them than you will find in Chapter 6. Fortunately, there other resources in which you can find deeper explanations. One very good source is the book *Joyful Path of Good Fortune, by Geshe Kelsang Gyatso.*

The nine levels describe ever-increasing powers of attention focused upon some virtuous mental content. As this is the Perfection of Concentration, the motivation of Bodhichitta/Godly loving is what results in the choice to engage in the practice of concentrating the mind. Bodhichitta/Godly loving, once acquired, always motivates a Bodhisattva/Godly lover. A mother looking at her child's eyes with her attention focused steadily upon her child's eyes is concentrating on the child's eyes. Feelings of love are always associated with this concentration. The mother most assuredly is looking at her child's eyes because of her love for the child. She is beholding her child as beloved and also looking at and into her child's eyes. The mother is reinforcing an interpersonal mental relationship of love between her and her child that she began to develop even before the child was born. Men do this, too.

The nine levels of concentration may be described as developing greater upon greater power to concentrate upon a mental content. With practice, the object of consciousness can be retained with increasing strength and focus and for longer periods of time. Any object a Bodhisattva/Godly lover has chosen to use as the focus of her or his attention has been chosen out of the motive of universal love. Bodhisattvas/Godly lovers love all sentient beings as a mother loves her child. Love is a relationship between conscious beings. When someone says, "I love potato chips," she or he is using the word *love* in the sense of lust. As most of the things we lust for cause us suffering rather than joy and peace of mind, most lust is utterly foolish. What Bodhisattvas and Godly lovers are trying to do is acquire Wisdom with a capital *W*—the Perfection of Wisdom—and this is the Wisdom of Love, not lusting for wisdom. For the remainder of this introduction, I will refer to Bodhisattvas and Godly lovers by the name *Lover* with a capital *L*. Since these are mere names and I am trying to help you, I ask you to please understand and accept this usage.

As I have explained, the perfections of Generosity, Patience, Effort, Moral Discipline, Concentration, and Wisdom are interconnected. I explained how Effort must attend all of the others and that a Lover can act both Generously and Patiently in one action if the Lover has acted intending to express both of these virtues through his or her action. Any level of increasing development of Concentration can be used to hasten development of any other perfection. We must understand that the process of giving birth to Wisdom requires both the father and the mother, just as every human must have both a biological father and a biological mother. Traditionally, the skills mastered in the first five Perfections are referred to as the method practices, and the skills mastered in the last Perfection, Wisdom, are referred to as the wisdom practices. Also, traditionally, the method practices are represented as expressing male powers, and the wisdom practices are represented as expressing female powers. Thus when I wrote that the process of giving birth to Wisdom requires both the father and the mother, you must understand that in order to acquire the Perfection of Wisdom, you must master both the method and the wisdom practices.

As an interim summary, Lovers use the perfection of Concentration to develop whatever perfection the Lover is trying to bring to full bloom by first bringing into being a content of mind that is helpful in achieving some purpose instrumentally useful for helping the Lover to achieve her or his ultimate purpose. When I was in high school many years ago, one very important purpose I had adopted at the time was to win high school football games for my school. My instrumental purposes for reaching this goal included smashing to the ground people who were trying to carry a ball across my goal line and by catching balls thrown to me by someone with whom I shared the purpose of carrying the ball across their goal line. I would think about my goals before falling asleep at night and at other times, and I would focus my mind on these goals of winning, stopping their crossing of our goal, and catching a ball and running across their goal. All of this seemed very exciting and meaningful to me at the time, and it helped me to be mildly successful in the very small environment of a few of the high school football fields of York County, Pennsylvania in 1966 and 1967.

I do not mean to disparage the role that sports can play in helping people to develop skills that will be useful in life. I just would like the skills that are developed to be useful in the pursuit of true and lasting happiness rather than hindrances to that pursuit. Whenever we want to achieve any goal, it is always helpful to concentrate on a mental image of our purpose as well as the purposes instrumentally useful for reaching our ultimate purpose. The Lover uses these same techniques, refining and developing them and calling these refined techniques meditation.

Meditation of the type I am talking about employs techniques for bringing to mind the features of a chosen meditation object, and when a clear enough mental content of that object arises, bringing the mind to focus on this object for as long as possible. The techniques used to cause the desired mental content to arise are called *analytical meditation,* and when the mind retains focus upon the desired mental content, this is called *placement meditation.* Usually when people in the West talk about meditation, they are talking about trying to bring calm to their mind by eliminating distracting and troubling thoughts. This may be called *calming meditation.* A mild form of joy always arises within a calm and peaceful mind. This is very important; please do not forget it. Calming meditation is not the perfection of Concentration; however, the perfection of Concentration cannot be acquired without a calm mind. We must calm our minds so as to develop Concentration, realizing that the pure joy of a calm mind arises in full measure when

Concentration comes to fruition at the ninth mental abiding with the object of focus upon the Ultimate Ground of All Things.

At this time, Madonna and Child immediately co-create the fruit of Wisdom: the joyful experience of union with the Ultimate Ground of All Things. You cannot just focus upon your breath and create the calm that is necessary to acquire Concentration and Wisdom. You have to first rid yourself of vicious thoughts, words, and deeds and replace them with the thoughts, words, and deeds that flow from universal, unbiased love. This is the Father method, which is also inextricably imbedded in the Madonna and Child relationship. This Father must never abandon the Woman who is Wisdom, because this Woman cannot give birth to Wisdom without His constant presence. No matter what your tradition is, as long as you think that we are suffering because of separation from the Holy and as long as you understand that to heal the separation, one must walk morally and seek the Wisdom of Love, then you can learn to see the Madonna and Child as expressing this metaphor.

In conclusion, the point of Chapter 6 is to give a short explanation of the process used by a Lover to develop the ability to focus her or his mind calmly upon a particular object. This object can be any object useful for developing any Perfection. In causing this object to arise in his or her mind, the Lover weaves his or her Loving into a very complicated set of conditions that jointly cause an object to arise in his or her mind. This Loving may be conceptually pulled for deeper inspection from this complicated fabric of causal conditions—but only conceptually pulled, as concepts are meaningless outside of a fabric of interconnected meanings. The Lover also weaves his or her ultimate purpose of achieving Wisdom—the final end of a human life, as Aristotle would say—into this causal fabric.

Part III

Chapter 7 of *Ocean of Compassion*

For the remainder of this introduction, I am going to use only the name *God* to talk about the meaning of Chapter 7. Advanced Bodhisattvas/Lovers will understand what I am saying no matter what word I use to talk about the content of a mind attending to the nature and Ultimate Ground of All Things, i.e. Emptiness.

There is a danger whenever a Lover tries to explain the nature of all things and their interrelationships through God's nature. The danger is that if a Lover attempts to explain God to someone whose mind is not properly prepared to understand God's nature, the person might enter into a suffer-causing chain of reasoning. So that you can understand how someone could fall into this suffer-causing chain of reasoning, I must explain to you three different concepts related to the word *existence.* These concepts are related in the sense of the middle and the two extremes.

The middle concept is the actual nature of God. God is the ground from which all things arise and to which all things return. God is never separated from anything; however, this does not mean that God is in everything. It is our ignorance of God's true nature that causes our separation from God. We are never really separated from God, and God is never really separated from us, but in our ignorance, we turn our eyes away from God and look at things rather than looking at God. You do not understand that your happiness is right here for your own inspection in the very life you are leading right now. Our problem is that we have separated ourselves from the God who is always everywhere.

Everyone always falls into one of the two extremes until the self-created separation from God is healed. God never turns away from us, but we are always turning away from God. We have created our own separation by using our minds to make illusory and meaningless things. By this I do not mean just things of idle diversion, such as playing cards, and objects of meaningless lust, such as fame and material wealth. I mean all things. We observe things arising all the time, and our mother teaches us to talk in a language that always uses "thing" words. This is no accident. It is because we have a mind that is innately erroneous. Even before mother teaches you to say *cow,* your mind constructs objects out of God's nature. When our mothers teach us to say *cow,* they point into God's undivided nature and say *cow.* This innate, erroneous thing-viewing is reinforced by the languages we speak. We can call this innate thing-making *innate self-grasping.*

We make both our self and other selves without having to convince ourselves that things exist. We just believe it. When this belief is questioned, we usually find a way to defend it, and the stories we tell about why selves/things must exist create intellectually-formed self-grasping. Philosophers have constructed incredibly impressive theoretical systems to try to fix problems they recognize in the concept of thingness/substance. Plato realized from Parmenides' teachings that we conceive of things as each having their own separate, undivided, unchanging, and uniform nature/essence. Plato then constructed a magnificent, unforgettable narrative entitled *The Republic* in which he pointed out that we all agree with Parmenides about the nature of a thing, but that what we observe in our daily lives aren't like this at all. He then went on to argue that we can find things like this but only in a Realm of Forms separate from the realm of our daily experience—the phenomenal world of our sense-based experiences. In the Realm of Forms, he wrote, one can find the undivided, unchanging and uniform things we all believe in.

What is actually true is that there is no Realm of Forms where we can find these separate things, but we do see them lurking in every thing we mentally make. Plato has probably written the greatest body of philosophical works that have yet been written, despite the stupendous error of constructing a Realm of Forms. Plato was brilliant in understanding that what Parmenides had said (i.e. that to be a thing is to possess an undivided, unchanging, and uniform nature) is what everybody believes about things and what everybody thinks he or she is seeing when beholding any object of consciousness. Plato's true brilliance unfolds in *The Parmenides,* in which he destroys the Realm of the Forms using the very reasoning process he said you have to teach Guardians to use to get to this realm. Plato knew when he wrote *The Parmenides* that things don't exist. He just had no idea how to develop this knowledge into the Wisdom of Love. He had no idea that there is such a thing as the Wisdom of Love.

I wrote that there is a danger involved when a Lover attempts to explain God's nature to someone. The danger in explaining God's nature to someone, which requires explaining that things don't exist in the way they appear to us, is that someone hearing this may conclude that nothing exists. This is called the extreme of nihilism, and a nihilist doesn't immediately die a physical death from believing that nihilism is true. However, nihilists can easily die a moral death. This is utter, complete, and disastrous self-separation from God. This is hell. You will read about some of the hells that can result from nihilism in Chapter 5. A Lover must be very careful to avoid saying stupid things that may result in nihilists going to hell.

The Middle Way is the understanding that God lies in the middle between the nonsense of things-separate and the nonsense of nihilism. God cannot be a thing-separate, because then God could not be the Ultimate Ground of All Things. But God is not in all things. The vastness that is called God cannot be put into anything—and most assuredly not into a group of non-existent things. I have now briefly described the general truth that God's nature is being the ground of all things. Being. I Am. Greeks could state a sentence with just the word *being.* We don't at the present time find true and lasting happiness in English. However, I use the technique of vowel-less sentences in Chapter 7. *Being* and *I Am* both express God's nature; however, the latter statement looks like God is saying, "I exist." Of course it is false that God doesn't exist. I have just finished explaining that God exists in the Middle Way. Being states God's nature succinctly in a better way than I Am does, because saying *Being* doesn't make God appear to be a thing. The word *God* does this, so we have to be very careful not to get trapped into believing that the Ground of All Things is a thing to be named using the word *God.*

Acquiring the perfection of Wisdom is an incredibly difficult intellectual struggle, but it always yields something very precious—happiness and the end of suffering. This is why the perfection of Wisdom is represented as a female figure. In Buddhism, her name is Prajnaparamita, which means the Perfection of Wisdom. Sophia is not a very common name anymore, but it is the Greek name of a metaphoric female wisdom figure. Sophia is one of the Greek roots that has been used to form the word *philosophy*—the love of wisdom. We all know that when a woman is in the process of giving birth, she has to endure a very difficult period of struggle. I suppose not all women think about the very difficult struggle they will have to endure when they choose to bring a baby into being, but I am sure a lot do. Although I haven't seen a scientific study saying this, I feel very confident that it is true that most women are aware of the difficult struggle that lies ahead and choose to undertake it because of being convinced the struggle is worth the result. I am trying to convince as many people as I can that the acquisition of the perfection of Wisdom is worth the struggle.

A mother wants to behold a preciousness that she knows she can only behold after a very difficult struggle. So she undertakes the responsibility of giving birth to this preciousness even though she will have to endure a very difficult and painful struggle. By this metaphor, you must understand the difficulty of the struggle required to give birth to Wisdom. The only metaphor that can come close to expressing the meaning of the struggle to acquire the perfection of Wisdom and of the preciousness that results is to depict Wisdom as a Mother with a newborn child. The metaphor is even deeper, because the concepts of mother and child are interrelated; their meanings are inextricably linked. Neither concept has any meaning without the other. The Perfection of Wisdom is a mother beholding a newborn child. This Woman—the Perfection of Wisdom—has chosen to bring Preciousness into the world. She has endured the difficult struggle to do this, and she is concentrating on the result of all of her labors with the full absorption of love. A blissful Madonna with Child is the pictorial metaphor for the Perfection of Wisdom. My wife and I have a silver relief that was made in Italy in our home, and the cover illustration of this book is my elder son's expression of this metaphor. The Italian Madonna and Child in our home is very meaningful to both my wife and to me; she thinks of herself as Christian, and I think of myself as Buddhist. It doesn't matter.

Now that you know the danger of nihilism as well as about the preciousness that results from acquiring the Perfection of Wisdom, let me begin the explanation of how one acquires this Perfection. Each of us has a mind that is aware of content. That is what mental functioning is. Mind and content are inextricably connected. If an observation of meaningful content is not occurring, then nothing mental is occurring. What is not so obvious and easy to understand is that neither the mind nor any of the contents of a mind is a thing. Kant, in *The Critique of Pure Reason,* argued that the only things we can experience are representations understood as mental contents, which he named *phenomena.* I agree that all we can have in our minds are mental objects. Kant said we can't know, but we should hope that there are real things outside our minds that our mental objects represent, as a photo represents something outside the photo. That is why he called them representations. Most of us don't merely hope that there are real things; we don't even consider the issue of whether what we experience are things. We then desperately seek to get things we think will make us happy. At least it is a start to move from an unquestioning belief in things to just hoping phenomena represent things. Really what we all want to do is figure out how to avoid suffering and acquire happiness, and we mistakenly think that the possession of things is necessary for us to succeed in these endeavors. But dare I repeat, "Do not store up for yourselves treasures on earth, where moth and rust consume and where thieves break in and steal; but store up for yourselves treasures in heaven, where neither moth nor rust consumes and where thieves do not break in and steal. For where your treasure is, there your heart will be also" (Matthew 6:19-21).

We need help to learn how to find true and lasting happiness. Very few people can figure this out without assistance. Everyone trying to sell you something is trying to convince you that he or she has something that will bring you some happiness or end some of your suffering, but true happiness and the total end of suffering result from achieving actual mental union with God. Everything else can only be helpful or hurtful to you in your quest to achieve this union. God must become an object of your direct consciousness in order for you to achieve lasting happiness and the end of all suffering. The sooner you do this, the better for all of us.

Let's return to the discussion of mental contents and minds so that I can explain how to make spiritual progress toward acquiring Wisdom so as to end the false separation from God we have created. As an example of mental content, if we say or think, "I see an apple," then the mind is attending to some content that carries the information that we are related to our environment such that we could act so as to try to have a mental content with the meaning, "This sure is a tasty, sweet, and crunchy fruit!" What that means can only be determined by understanding how the thinker/speaker is trying to relate to his or her environment. Our environments include other conscious beings relating themselves to their environments and using information transmission to share meaning with one another. Statements do not get their meaning by denotation, which is to say, their meanings do not arise as a result of conscious beings naming events out there. What is happening is that we learn to say, "This sure is a tasty, crunchy apple!" by learning how other English speakers attempt to relate themselves to their environments in ways which we understand by analogy to how we are trying to relate ourselves to our environments. You do not have to speak a human language in order to do this.

Minds, mental contents, meanings, and environments arise within a complicated mind-content-meaning development-information gathering-information sharing process. The point of developing the perfection of Concentration is to help us develop this complex process so that we can achieve a relationship with our environment that results in the mental content of union with God. Everyone can achieve this union, and it is achieved through placement meditation on the inescapable truth that things don't exist in the way we perceive them to exist, i.e. as things-separate from each other, separate from God, and separate from being a mental content. Because of the difficulty of actually understanding and accepting this inescapable Truth with sufficient depth so as to break the innate habit of thing-making, one must have a tremendously powerful motivation to undertake the struggle to know this Truth. A motivation of sufficient power to succeed in this struggle can only come from understanding the infinite preciousness to be found at the end of the struggle and having the boundless love that Jesus and Buddha told us we must have. Jesus did not say, "It is a lovely but unreachable ideal to love everybody to the same degree as you love yourself, so try to love a few people a bit more thoroughly." He said, "Love the Lord your God with all your heart, all your soul, all your mind, and all your strength. The second is this, 'Love your neighbor as yourself.' There is no commandment greater than these" (Mark 12:30-31). Is there something unclear about that? This is the motivation I am telling you that you must have if you are to succeed in the infinitely valuable goal of healing your separation from God.

The perfection of Wisdom arises after one perfects the ability to rest the mind on the conclusion, "There is neither a me-thing in here nor any non-me-things out there, because there are no things whatsoever." The aim is to see things as they really are—as mental contents that have been given meanings through the process of naming. We are trying to bring into the mind-content relationship the process of the arising of the illusion of the existence of self-identifiable things. Buddha, who loved everyone in exactly the same way as Jesus did, taught that we are creating the things of waking consciousness in almost the same way as we do when we create things in our dreaming consciousness. The only difference between the things of dreams and things of waking consciousness is the sorts of things we appeal to when we explain to ourselves and to one another how the mental content of a thing out there arose. In dreams, we appeal to things that we believe are in our internal environment—such as memories, hopes, fears, wishes, unconscious beliefs, and so forth—and we say that the mind just made up objects containing meanings related to these things. When we talk about waking experiences, we appeal to things not just in our internal environment, but we also must appeal to things we believe are in an external environment. However, environments do not come from things.

As I explained earlier, environments arise out of interdependent relationships, and relationships are not things, although we can talk about them as if they were things. Immanuel Kant realized that things are made by mind, but he thought that it was necessary to show that the things of waking consciousness are different from the things of dreams, because he—like just about everybody—believed that there really must be things out there. He thought that if there aren't things out there, then waking consciousness would be just idle dreams, as if dreams have no meaning whatsoever. Of course dreams have meanings, so they are not idle; it's just that it is not easy to understand the meaning of dreams. It is easier to understand how we are using the things we think are out there to help us relate to our environments.

Kant distinguished between phenomena, which he acknowledged are contents of mind, and things-in-themselves, which he said must be out there in order for our phenomena to be meaningful, or in his words, not just idle dreams. He named these hoped-for external things *noumena.* It is not necessary for there to be noumena in order for our waking phenomena to be meaningful. Kant believed that what the mind does is to structure information coming to us from out there through our senses into objects that he hoped represented the things out there. This is not what is happening; there is only the process in which mental content arises within the mind-content-environment-meaning making-information sharing process. We can try to describe this process in words, but words always talk about things, so an inter-relationship process cannot be described adequately in words. But minds do not have to have contents that always carry thing-meaning, despite what Kant claimed. He believed that the mind always structures what he thought was coming from out there into things. He said that the mind always uses the category of substance in creating phenomenal experience. Substance is the mind engaging in the process of thing-naming. Although we all realize that there is a big difference between apples and thinking about Chicago, our only way of talking about this latter mental content turns the mental content into an internal thing, "the about-Chicago thought."

Now that I have briefly described this process of mental content formation, I can explain the purpose and expand upon the meanings expressed in Chapters 6 and 7. What is going on in these chapters is an attempt for me to both understand and transmit the information contained in the answer to the question, "How does one come to have as a mental content the Ultimate Ground of All Things, i.e. God?" Well, the short answer is that the process of coming to have this content begins by understanding that the true nature of things is that there aren't any things. Although this may sound completely ridiculous, I believe that this notion is not only imbedded in the scriptures of Buddhism, but also imbedded in the scriptures of monotheistic religions. "The Fall" is a falling away from the ultimate reality of God; it is a separation from God that we have created, and so we are faced with the task of bringing ourselves back into right relationship with God in order to end the separation we have created and are perpetuating through our own errors.

The Adam and Eve story is a metaphor, not a description of events in which person-things called Adam and Eve separated themselves from the person-thing called God. For someone who believes that this story is literally true, it would be difficult—but not impossible—to understand the meaning of Chapter 7. On the other hand, someone who understands this story as a metaphorical expression of the self-caused separation from God that needs to be healed can more easily undertake the challenge of repairing the rift. The meaning of the separation cannot adequately be communicated in words because words always create things. "In the beginning was the Word." (John 1: 1) The beginning is not the beginning of time; it is the beginning of the separation. God, to people who understand this meaning, is not some guy sitting on a throne in a place called heaven; rather, God is the underlying reality of all things, the source of all things, and the reality from which things arise and to which things return. This is a reality that is not just the source of all things, but a reality expressing loving-kindness.

There is a long tradition of mysticism in Christianity, Judaism, and Islam, and what mystics have been trying to do is the same thing Buddhists are trying to do. People who don't understand what mysticism is think that mystics are trying to bring about some kind of ecstatic experience that is only different from a drug-induced ecstatic experience in the explanation of how the ecstatic experience arose. Mystics are not trying to bring about an ecstatic experience. They are trying to bring their minds into contact with the underlying reality from which they come. It just so happens to be true that if someone is successful in doing this, he or she experiences what Buddhists call bliss and Christians call ecstasy. Neither monotheistic mystics nor Buddhists are trying to achieve bliss. They are trying to achieve union with God. The only difference is that within Buddhism, the methods are more thoroughly and completely articulated than I have seen within the monotheistic religions. Maybe there are secret teachings within these traditions of which I am not aware that are this thorough and complete. If so, I don't think these methods should be kept secret. All that has to be done is to first carefully prepare the audience so that the trap of nihilism is avoided. The short explanation of the method to use so as to achieve union with God is that, from the motivation of Jesus-like loving, one must struggle to bring the mind to rest on the conclusion that the separation of self from God is a mind-made illusion.

In order to develop the Perfection of Wisdom, one ponders the reasons why the separation is only a self-made illusion, and one employs the Perfection of Concentration to bring one's mind to rest on this conclusion until the separation of the world into you and not you dissolves. There are two aspects of meditation that have to be employed in order to overcome the separation—analytic meditation and placement meditation. In analytic meditation, you either review the reasons why some statement is true or you review and attempt to visualize the features of a meditational figure. As an example of a meditational figure, Buddhists use Tara, a compassionate and loving, female, Jesus-like figure. A Christian could, obviously, visualize Jesus. Monotheistic traditions that do not have figures such as this to visualize must use reasoning-based analytic meditations only. Analytic-meditation methods lead to the arising of the desired mental content within the mind of the person doing meditation—Godly loving, for example. The second form of meditation is called placement meditation. In placement meditation, one holds the mind resting in focus upon the mental content that arises in analytic meditation. When one fully develops placement meditation from the motivation of universal loving, one has acquired the Perfection of Concentration. Chapter 6, as previously explained, describes the levels of development one passes through on the way to developing the Perfection of Concentration.

Buddhists may use a visualization of Tara to practice the Perfection Concentration, or they may use a virtuous feeling such as love or compassion, for example. A Mahayana Buddhist would bring to mind the representational appearance of Tara in analytic meditation so as to form a mental image of Tara and then hold the mind at rest, focused upon the visualization of Tara. Because one knows that Tara represents universal love and compassion, bringing one's mind to rest on the mental image of Tara can help to develop this kind of love as long as both the image and the understanding of what the image represents are parts of the mental content you have brought the mind to rest upon.

The other kind of analytic meditation—reviewing the reasons why some statement is true or just recalling repetitively the words expressing the belief that some statement is true—can also bring about the change in your mind that is your goal. Rather than visualizing something that represents universal love and compassion, you can review the reasons why you should become a person who loves in the way Jesus said we should love and/or think about words that express this way of loving. When feelings of conviction and/or love arise, one then does placement meditation upon the convictions/feelings that have arisen. Doing this repeatedly over time results in the achievement of the goal you have sought to reach. The verses in Chapter 1 can be used in analytic-to-placement meditation in the way I have just described. To overcome the faulty separation of ourselves from God, one must employ Concentration with the mind focused upon the Truth that this separation is erroneous. In the end, only analytic meditation upon this Truth and the reasons why it is true can overcome the separation.

The reasons presented in Chapter 7 distinguish between two kinds of truth—the truth we assign to the statements we use in our ordinary day-to-day lives and the Truth that we must assign to the statement that all of these statements are ultimately false. The statements we ordinarily use in our day-to-day lives when we communicate with one another are false for two reasons. Every one of them asserts that things-separate exist, and these statements are asserted in a language which is utterly inconsistent. The only truths that we have good reason to assert in these languages are those which are instrumentally helpful to us in achieving the happiness and the elimination of suffering that are possible as a result of overcoming our false separation from God. Quite a lot of what we say can fit into this understanding that our languages are only instrumentally useful. The statements we make to convince ourselves and others that happiness can be achieved merely through the possession of things and the achievement of mere worldly goals are all completely wrong and foolish.

In Chapter 7, The Guardian and Ella are characters in a narrative in which The Guardian is helping guide Ella to a philosophical understanding of Emptiness. Ella is a young girl who is a reincarnation of Immanuel Kant. Ella knocks on The Guardian's door in a state of amnesia, but she has memories that have led her to believe that she is a reincarnation of Immanuel Kant. Even if you don't believe in reincarnation, it can still be fun to think about what would happen if Kant were to be reincarnated in the form of a young girl and then got stuck in a situation in which she has to listen to and discuss philosophy with a group of contemporary philosophers. Annette Baier and Richard Rorty are the contemporary philosophers in this narrative, and Erwin Schrödinger appears in a cameo role. The Mother in the narrative is the personification of the Perfection of Wisdom. If you don't know about the Schrödinger Cat analogy, you will have to read about it to understand why Erwin Schrödinger is present. The Guardian acquires this name because he or she answered Ella's knock and guards and guides her.

Annette Baier and Richard Rorty are characters who represent the philosophical commitments of Annette Baier and Richard Rorty. Annette Baier currently lives in New Zealand and was a Professor of Philosophy at the University of Pittsburgh for many years, including the time during which I studied there and eventually earned my PhD in philosophy. Annette's character tells Ella that Kant's theory of what it is to be a person is mistaken and silly. She informs Ella of a different, interconnected understanding of what it is to be a person that is in harmony with the interconnectedness of all that I outlined above. Neither The Guardian nor The Mother ever challenges what Annette says.

Richard Rorty, at the time of the writing of this book, is deceased, but he was a professor of philosophy at a number of universities, including Princeton University. Richard Rorty believed and argued that there is no such thing as objective truth. He held the view that all truth is conventional and arises in dependence upon how groups of people communicate with one another. According to this view, truth always arises within the context of agreement between humans about what sentences are true and what sentences are false. According to Rorty, humans find the meaning and truth of sentences in basically the same way as I have described how meaning arises. However, Rorty believed that was the end of the story. He did not believe that our way of communication creates a separation between self and non-self that is erroneous. He eventually came to espouse a pragmatic criterion of conventional truth, as I have above, but he did not articulate the belief that the ultimate pragmatic goal is to overcome separation from God and reach true and lasting happiness.

One strategy for arguing that ultimately there are no things is to argue of each particular thing or class of things that it is not possible for that thing or class of things to exist as a thing-separate. The problem with this strategy is that over time, people believe in the existence of different things. Also, given the large number of things and types of things people believe exist, it is not reasonable to claim that you have proved that no things exist as long as some other type of thing or particular thing could be asserted to exist, which can always be done. The Guardian adopts a strategy intended to show that all claims that things exist are made in a language that is necessarily inconsistent and that all claims that a thing exists lead to paradox. These are two different arguments ad absurdum. If a statement leads to inconsistency and/or paradox, that is a sufficient reason to conclude that the statement is false from the ultimate point of view. It is not necessary to argue of any particular thing that it doesn't exist if it can be shown that thing commitments lead to inconsistency and/or paradox. This is the strategy that The Guardian adopts to argue that no things exist from the ultimate point of view. However, thing talk can still be pragmatically useful if we have the correct pragmatic criterion of truth, as outlined in the immediately preceding paragraph.

The main philosophical arguments of Chapter 7 are in the dialogue between The Guardian and Richard Rorty regarding Richard Rorty's merely conventional theory of truth, wherein The Guardian presents the theory that there are two different trues—conventional true and Ultimate True. The Guardian has two strategies to argue that there are these two different kinds of truth. Ultimate Truth is not conventional. However, The Guardian prefers not to call it Objective Truth. This expression seems to carry with it the notion that the reason Truth is not conventional is because some statements successfully refer to real objects and events, but the Guardian denies that this why Ultimate Truth is not conventional truth.

Obviously, each of the following three claims requires a proof: "There is both a conventional true and an Ultimate True." "It is Ultimately True is that all conventional statements are false." "Thing talk always leads to paradox." The arguments embedded in the narrative of Chapter 7 are intended to prove these claims. The arguments in defense of these claims are interrelated but separate. First, The Guardian argues that it is not a silly idea to break the concept of truth into two types. The Guardian defends that this idea does not create a silly mess of destroying the unity of meaning of the word *truth.* The Guardian argues that we can and must make a distinction between conventional truth and Ultimate Truth in a way that is analogous to how the concept of number has been divided into two types based upon the distinction between real and imaginary numbers. Most people do not even know that there are numbers that fall into the imaginary type, much less know that imaginary numbers are very useful. In the set of real numbers, when you square a number, you always get a positive number. Both one multiplied by one and minus one multiplied by minus one equal one, and so on for all of the real numbers. On the other hand, there are numbers such that when you square a negative number of this type, you get a negative number. The set of these numbers are called the imaginary numbers, and one times i is the name of the first integer in the set of imaginary numbers, whereas one is the first integer in the set of real numbers.

The theory of numbers does not have a split personality, because these two sets of numbers sets intersect at zero. There is not a real zero and a different imaginary zero. A unified theory of numbers is maintained, because by multiplying any real number—say two by i—you get an imaginary number that is ordered in the same way as the real numbers are ordered. You get one i followed by two i, and so on.

The Guardian claims that if we divide truth in an analogous way, we still retain an underlying unity of inter-relationship between the two truths. Most people think that there is one true, one false, and that is it. There are a lot of logic specialists, i.e. logicians, who do not accept that there are only two truth values known as true and false. The idea that there is only true and false is abandoned by these logicians, because if there is only true and false and with it we assess the truth and falsity of statements, some really big problems result.

One problem with our conventional concept of truth occurs when an inconsistency exists within a set of statements, each of which is assigned as either true or false. From arguments using the rules widely accepted and imbedded within the reasoning most people use, we can prove anything from a set that has just one pair of inconsistent statements. An inconsistency arises in an argument (that is statements being put forth as stating reasons, the premise[s], to show that another statement, the conclusion, is true) when the premises of that argument contain a statement *S,* and the premises assert both "S is true" and "S is false." From this inconsistent pair and using our common rules of reasoning, one can prove any statement at all using these rules. For example, you could prove—if you wanted to—the statement, "At this very moment, the sun at the center of our solar system is both shining and not shining everywhere on earth." Another example of a statement you could prove would be the statement, "It is true that I am now eating a red apple, and it is false that I am now eating a red apple." As computers are programmed using this logic—and it is usually the case that inconsistencies are imbedded within the information computers process—various techniques are used to stop computers from giving us information that is inconsistent nonsense. From just one statement asserting this kind of inconsistent nonsense, you can then go on to prove that every statement in the whole system is both true and false. This kind of system is called *explosively inconsistent,* because as soon as one inconsistency crops up, the whole language system blows up into the assignment of both true and false to every statement in the system. The point of all of this is that using our normal logical rules—that is to say the rules of reasoning that almost everybody uses and with which our computers are programmed—from only one bit of inconsistent information, you can logically derive every actual and possible statement anyone may care to prove.

If computers crunched out this kind of inconsistent information all the time, they wouldn't be of much use to us as we attempt to organize our mind-content-meaning-information gathering—information sharing interrelationships, so various strategies have been adopted to prevent our computers from spitting out nonsense if the information they are processing is inconsistent. This can happen anytime complex information about the observations people have made about their relationships with their environments is entered into a computer. Obviously the meanings people derive from their differing interrelationships with their environments are different, and often times they certainly look quite different and are quite frequently expressed using sentences that, as stated, are contradictory. We want our computers to help us understand the complexity of this information, not tell us that every possible statement you can think of is true. Of course, what I hope for is that we can learn how to use our computers to help us repair the separation we have created between ourselves and God and not just make it easier for us to do nonsensical things.

The conventional truth that is embedded in our natural languages must lead to explosive inconsistency in the system, because we can understand the meaning of the statement, "This sentence is false." It says, of itself, that it is false. If this self-referential sentence is accepted as true, then since it truly states that it is false, the statement is false. If this self-referential sentence is false, then since it states that it is false, the sentence is true. In either case, an inconsistent pair of sentences is generated. With only the conventional truth that is embedded in our natural languages, this problem cannot be blocked. Because of this problem and the problem that computers will likely contain inconsistencies whenever given a large amount of information to process, logicians have tried to come up with a many-valued logic and/or have attempted to abandon the law of non-contradiction in order to deal with the problem of an explosive inconsistency within natural languages. The previous attempts at creating a many-valued logic have been of limited success in assisting in the computer analysis of sets containing inconsistent statements, and abandoning the law of non-contradiction within the context of merely the one type of truth—conventional truth—means it is okay to say both "I am eating a red apple right now" and "I am not eating a red apple right now."

This is silly, but we can have it both ways by distinguishing between the conventional true and the Ultimate True.

The separate me's we create normally either don't notice or simply dismiss information that is inconsistent with other beliefs we have and cling to. We often assign "true" to statements expressing the meanings we attach to the beliefs we are clinging to and "false" to those which contradict these meanings so as to keep inconsistencies out of our meaning system. But also, often people are content to hold on to a set of inconsistent beliefs even when the inconsistency is pointed out to them and even if they reason in such a way that from contradictory premises one could prove anything. What is happening is that they are ignoring the inconsistency and continuing to interact with their environment in ways that can still be described meaningfully. However, the fear is that if we don't find a way to deal with these inconsistencies so as to stop the derivation of any statement at all from inconsistent premises, then meaning would collapse into meaninglessness. If this were to happen, the ability to interact with an environment would collapse, and presumably, we would all then die as a result of our confusion. Obviously, we are still here despite the fact that we hold inconsistent beliefs. However, we do need to find a way to keep our computers from spitting out meaningless nonsense from inconsistent premises if they are to be useful to us in our attempts to repair our separation from God.

At the present time, computers are programmed using numbers to assign truth values to the information being processed. The simplest way to do this is to assign 1 to true and 0 to false. Unfortunately, as discussed above, from inconsistent information, this can lead to logical disaster and the resultant meaningless information coming from our computers. Strategies such as assigning ½ true to both of two conflicting statements have been adopted to deal with the contradictory information computers are being used to process. I do not think that this is very helpful to understanding the relationship between conventional true and Ultimate True.

The Guardian makes the argument that natural languages are explosively inconsistent because since conventional true is embedded in every natural language, the inconsistency that arises from the statement "This statement is false" cannot be blocked from arising in any natural language. Because of this, from the plane of Ultimate True, all statements in natural languages are false, whereas from the plane of conventional true, all statements are both true and false, so we can only choose pragmatically between statements in our assignment of the conventional values true and false. All statements in natural languages have subjects, and most have objects, so every statement says something like, "The apple I am eating is red." The philosopher Bertrand Russell argued that all statements like this are making an existence claim. He said their meaning is to be analyzed as asserting, "There exists some particular thing, x, and x is an apple and x is red." The Guardian agrees. The upshot is that, since all of these statements are false, from the ultimate point of view, none of the things to which the statements purport to make reference exist. By placing and holding one's mental focus on this conclusion with the perfection of Concentration, one can achieve the Supreme Mind of Union and heal the false separation from God.

The Guardian next reminds Richard of the paradox of the heap. This paradox goes like this: One grain of sand is not a heap. Adding another non-heap to a non-heap does not make a heap, and so on. Thus, one can never add enough grains of sand to other grains of sand to make a heap thing. The Guardian points out that every single thing we talk about is analogous to a heap; all things are made up of parts, each of which is not what it is to be the thing being created in being named. This goes for physical objects as well as abstract objects such as space, time, love, hate, distance, and so on. Since using sentences that refer to heaps can be pragmatically useful, it is okay to say that from the conventional point of view there are heaps. But from the ultimate point of view, there are no heaps. All heaps arise from our conventional naming-observing activities. You may reflect upon the Schrödinger's Cat analogy to reinforce this. Again, by concentrating on the conclusion that things don't exist, one can develop the Supreme Mind of Union and heal the false separation from God.

The Guardian claims that the solution to the pragmatic problem of computing from a set of inconsistent statements is to make use of the division of truth into conventional truth and Ultimate Truth. Just as the separate planes of real and imaginary numbers intersect at zero, the planes of conventional truth and Ultimate Truth intersect at false. Just as there is only one zero, there is only one false. Computer programmers use 1 to represent true and 0 to represent false, except in those cases where a multi-value truth system is used to deal with the problem of explosive inconsistency. The Guardian says we should use 1 to represent conventional true, 0 to represent false, and 1i to represent Ultimate True. From the point of view of Ultimate Truth, all conventional truths get assigned 0. From the point of view of conventional truth, we may assign true or false values to whatever we have good pragmatic reason to assign true or false, and we thereby block explosive inconsistency. The paradox of the heap is also solved by dividing truth into conventional true and Ultimate True, because although it is Ultimately True that there are no heaps, we can use the conventional name *heap* in any way that we find pragmatically useful.

Tenzin Norbu
Omaha, Nebraska
September 2011

Chapter 1

Cultivating Bodhichitta

A precious human life,
Gateway to your final design,
Is the finest chance to progress we can have;
Don't waste this cherished time.

Bodhichitta is the supreme jewel of practice;
It impels us down the path.
Without the proper motivation,
Our happiness will not last.

The mind of respected Bodhichitta is
Exquisite and rare to find.
So earnestly strive with your sweetest Effort
To cultivate this mind.

All the suffering that we endure
In this precious human span
Arises from cherishing only ourselves and
Spurning the others at hand.

Why must suffering be avoided?
No answer do we need.
As we want to end our own,
To all others, pay heed.

The act of relieving the pain of one person
Shows a limited kind of care.
Act so as to snuff out suffering;
With all others, your love, do share.

I am just one lone existence;
All others are numberless.
Aim to achieve the bliss of each being, and
Your steps will always be blessed.

Friends, enemies, and strangers—
These collections are not permanent.
Empty each class; place the former members
In the class of equal deference.

Recall that a child naturally acts to
Help a mother in distress.
Consider everyone as former mothers.
Assist all; give nothing less.

Develop love universal;
Ponder the kindness of all.
Without the help received from others,
We would have nothing at all.

We praise a kindness to repay
A prior kindness done.
Far greater is the merit earned when acting only with the thought
To help another one.

We are bothered by and want to end
The pain of those we adore.
The kinship we feel gives us a motive;
Their sufferings we abhor.

We feel akin to those viewed as like us;
Reflect on the likeness we bear
To each other as fellows who suffer.
A connection with all, we share.

So put yourself in the place of all others;
Their feelings of woe you will know.
Your new self will want to bar all suffering.
To the end of the path you'll go.

When Bodhichitta has bathed your mind,
Never forsake this aim.
With this ambition, you'll dispel your suffering; for
Others you'll do the same.

Boundless love arises but rarely;
It's a precious jewel-like mind.
Its birth is always a matchless wonder—
A peerless and treasured find.

The benefits of this jewel of a mind
Are profound and measureless.
All suffering ends, joy comes to each person,
All happiness comes to pass.

The moment you generate Bodhichitta, into
Buddha's lineage you're born.
You enter the gateway to the Mahayana
And help all those forlorn.

A Bodhisattva earns veneration
From humans and all gods.
You surpass all hearers and distant achievers on
The path they've never trod.

You easily accumulate countless merit; powerful
Defects are soon cleansed.
You fulfill all of your virtuous desires; to
Vice you never tend.

Wearing the armor of Bodhichitta, you're
Kept safe from harms that befall.
Spiritual grounds and paths are accomplished;
Joy and peace you bring to all.

When in the grip of awesome fear,
We want to find a guard.
Bodhichitta, we know, can always protect us;
We'll find no danger hard.

Just as a star, exploding, consumes
All objects in its domain,
Bodhichitta destroys all vices;
Only virtues will remain.

A marigold flowers only one year,
And then it surely must die.
Bodhichitta flourishes constantly;
Upon it you must rely.

Bodhichitta abides in two precious ways;
Keep both of these in mind.
The goal to become a Buddha for all
Is what we first must find.

But having a goal bereft any Effort
Will always leave us behind.
With Effort seek the goal in practice;
Employ the engaging kind.

Just as the difference between wishing to go and
Truly going is known,
Strive to possess the two Bodhichittas;
Both of them must be shown.

The aspiration gives rise to
Limited freedom from pain.
But engaging in the exalted actions
Is an endless source of gain.

Adopt the Bodhisattva's deeds;
Powerful merit results.
Credit flows without interruption
And washes away your faults.

All living beings strive to end suffering, but
Blindly cause it to come.
Wishing happiness, but alas, in confusion,
They never bring it home.

Those who suffer, afflicted with sorrow, have a
Balm to heal their wounds.
Bodhisattvas offer to all protection
Like a mother's womb.

Nowhere else can there be found
Friends with virtue such as this.
None lacking it can be their equals; they
Pull us back from the abyss.

When Bodhisattvas encounter
Any trouble at all,
Only virtues are developed,
Upon them they stand tall.

A Bodhisattva brings his mind
To rest in joyful Concentration.
This penultimate attainment
Quickly escorts all to salvation.

A Bodhisattva will then eschew
Ignorant grasping at any self.
This success allows her to
All others render propitious help.

No words can ever fairly express
The Bodhisattva's worth
From constantly acting just for others to
End their terrible curse.

To all of those who have this aim, I express devotion;
That I owe this is a fact.
I can only give to them prostrations,
As there's nothing they could lack.

Chapter 2

The Engaging Bodhichitta of Effort

Sages have said that, among the Perfections,
Effort is thought to be best.
When we take delight in acting with virtue,
We will achieve all the rest.

Wishing to help all sentient beings
Puts Bodhichitta in play.
Engaging in deeds, with joy, that actually help
Is Effort's benevolent way.

Effort provides a counter to
The threefold forms of sloth.
The first of these, procrastination, causes
Delay upon the path.

Time passes quickly; chances are lost.
Life's duration is unknown.
Deploy Effort now; evade the traps:
An example for all is shown.

Please know the second form of sloth:
The attractions we must skirt.
Meaningless and nonvirtuous acts
Are the doings to avert.

These worldly enjoyments are like a flame,
And we are like a moth.
The wheel of woe tightly entraps us as we
Fly toward the holocaust.

Discouraging doubt is the third form of sloth,
And it takes away our delight.
We must counter our doubts to restore joy in virtue
With all our Bodhisattva might.

Discouragement with the pace of our progress
Leads us to guess that our aim
Is too high for us—perhaps even foolish.
Effort must parry this shame.

Doubts about the existence of Buddhas
With the perfection they have found
Can dishearten us in our practice,
And to samsara we'll be bound.

Flaws we perceive in our Spiritual Guide,
The Sangha and Spiritual Friends,
Can dampen the desire we have for the path, and
Away from our practice we tend.

The basis of all these discouraging doubts
Is rooted in what we perceive.
We assume that what we do not espy
Is something that cannot be.

But daily, we see illusions,
And first think real things do occur.
Still, knowledge of outer and inner errors
Can lead us these thoughts to abjure.

What appears to the mind actually comes
From the workings of mind itself.
Recall that a mind of confusion
Often fails to see what can help.

Strive with Effort to acquire Wisdom;
Then, with this knowledge, you can see
A purity that arises from practicing dharma,
And a Buddha too you will be.

Just as sloth can be seen in three forms,
Effort, too, is ternate.
Put on your armor, gather virtuous dharmas,
Benefit all in your wake.

With armor-like effort, we never give up,
No matter the hardships we dispute.
Be determined; cultivate the whole path.
Bodhichitta bears wonderful fruit!

Generate armor-like effort upon taking your vows;
Bodhisattvas never resign.
Begin each morning with armor-like effort;
Resolve to persist through all time.

Armor-like effort attends all the others.
Without it, no progress is made.
When you wear this armor continuously,
The vows you have taken won't fade.

Gathering virtuous dharmas through acting with merit
Employs the aims Discipline casts.
Take joy in practices that evince Moral Discipline;
Your journey on the path will last.

The effort of benefiting others
Makes Bodhichitta your craft.
The mere desire to bring aid to others
Is shallow; make love your task.

To improve your Effort, there are four powers.
Please strive to employ each kind.
Maintain aspiration; stay steadfast;
Be relaxed; keep a joyful mind.

The power of aspiration
Has a scrupulous aim unique.
We possess this power fully
When virtue is all that we seek.

Maintain aspiration through deep contemplation;
Reflect on the blessings received
By yourself, but more so, all others,
When the virtue you seek is achieved.

Maintain aspiration through deep contemplation;
Reflect on karmic offshoots.
Negative deeds, too, plant karmic seeds; sow to
Reap only delightful fruit.

Brief bursts of practice are like a waterfall
Engendered by a storm.
Steadfast power flows like a river:
Gently, continuously, stably. It's firm.

Relaxation is a power that
Conserves and supports our pleasure.
Slow down when needed before new endeavors.
Feel refreshed, renewed, and treasured.

If our practice is a source of delight,
With happiness we play.
As the Six Perfections lead all to bliss,
You can know them this way.

Athletes are elated when scoring a goal;
This prize is proudly held dear,
But the virtuous deeds of a Bodhisattva
Score the True Goal—ending fear.

So practice Dharma like a child at play;
You'll be joyfully at ease.
Neither acutely excited nor sadly dejected,
You and all others are pleased.

In order for Effort to do its work,
We always must guard our own mind.
Employ mindfulness and alertness.
Be aware; assess what you find.

Just as a sentry guarding a gate
Must observe to protect what he prizes,
Employ the guard of mindfulness;
Carefully watch for all that arises.

Just as the sentry must check and see
To determine if friend or foe,
Employ the guard of alertness:
Whether virtue or vice, she'll know.

Carefully observe all phenomena.
Be alert for the root delusions.
Anger, attachment, and ignorance
Must be shed to halt all illusions.

Rebirth in unfortunate realms
Does not come from body or speech.
It comes from mind; clear it of vice:
The goal that you seek will be reached.

An action that accords with virtue
Can only have a fortunate result
When the mind is not distracted elsewhere.
Keep it focused on the act without fault.

When thoughts counter to virtue arise,
Impassive you always should be.
Each vicious act that you avoid
Brings you closer to victory.

Spur yourself on to avoid harmful thoughts;
Recall Buddhas see all and are present.
As a child avoids disappointing a parent,
Insure your thoughts are, to them, most pleasant.

Carefully listen to and study Dharma
With respect and Bodhichitta.
Dharma is the supreme remedy
For grasping and anathema.

We have achieved this human life
After countless nativity.
Hold fast to your final intention with Effort.
Make it firm, stable, and steady.

Upon encounter with each living being,
Recall the good you gather in
From depending upon these sentient friends:
Full enlightenment you can win.

If you find the opportunity to teach,
Impart with only a pure intention.
Maintain the motive of Bodhichitta;
Don't merely seek wealth or reputation.

Explain Dharma to all those who listen
With a clear and double aim.
Strive to lead them to liberation,
For Buddhahood do the same.

This human body we have attained is
Quite fit for spiritual progression.
No other reason supports cherishing it.
It's a mere temporary collection.

Regard your body as a boat to take
All to the farther shore.
Accomplish the welfare of all living beings;
Effort can do no more.

Earnestly practice purification
Employing the fourfold forces:
Regret, reliance, the opponent force, and the
Pledge to curb future poor choices.

If we don't regret the wrongs we have done,
How can we possibly cleanse?
We remain inclined to continue to err,
And our suffering won't end.

In purification, we rely upon
Bodhichitta and the three precious gems.
Go for refuge; bring to mind your great aim:
The opponent force you employ will cleanse.

Superb opponent forces are known:
Vajrasattva and the Three Heaps.
Employ these practices every day
Then make a pledge that you can keep.

Having applied the other three powers,
It is time to promise to cease
Acting with error in the future
For as long as we can surcease.

With the pleasure of Effort, I must watch carefully
The elephant of my mind—
Keep it tied to the post of mindfulness
So it won't rampage and grind.

We fight to avoid a physical wound of the
Most trifling consequence.
But any wound self-inflicted on mind can crush us
Like a mammoth immense.

We must routinely prescribe the perfections
As doctors daily care for our weal.
But little is accomplished just by reciting the words.
With Effort, our prescription will heal.

Chapter 3

The Engaging Bodhichitta of Generosity

The Bodhisattva's practice of Giving is
A perfection of body, speech, and mind.
Mind forms a virtuous intention to give;
Body and speech bestow gifts of their kind.

Just as with the other perfections,
The intention must be pure.
Ensure the mind of Bodhichitta leads;
Of the correct aim you can be sure.

Giving has a result to hold dear:
Something profound is gathered in.
The same is true of all the first five.
The collection of merit begins.

We can develop our power to give,
Reflecting on karmic outcomes not holy.
But the Bodhisattva only attends, when Giving,
To the exemplary deed itself solely.

Acts of Giving have a clear result;
Future abundance is our fate.
This allows us to gather even more merit
By Giving when more is at stake.

If the merit Bodhisattvas gain from Giving
Were into grains of sand transmuted,
The countless granules in an endless dessert
Don't equal the merit they're imputed.

Bodhisattvas even give away
All the merit they have amassed.
When the merit has been passed to others,
They continue to love—hold fast.

By gathering abundant merit,
Full Buddahood we can accomplish.
So collecting this great treasure trove
Helps us satisfy everyone's wish.

Giving and the other perfections
Are accompanied by good cheer.
In this way, Effort is always present,
And success comes year by year.

A giver imparts three types of gift;
Each has its purpose and place.
Bodhisattvas display Giving of each type.
Boundless love fills all of space.

Of the three forms of gift we can give,
One is material things.
When we combine this with both of the others,
Good fortune to all we bring.

One of the tangible things we can give
Is an admired article we own.
Grasping the palpable goods we possess
Cannot bring happiness; this is well-known.

Every tangible item we buy
Will eventually disappear.
So, how can clenching things ephemeral
Bring us that which is lasting and dear?

If, instead, we practice giving away
Things acquired because we have been blessed
As a result of past acts of bestowing,
Real meaning comes from all of this largess.

The wealth we possess has come to us
From our Giving, not our greed.
When possessing this worldly asset,
Apply it to help those in need.

Although we usually give
To those who come from our seed,
It's a far greater meritorious deed
To give to those most in need.

If we have just a few possessions,
We still can shower with gifts
A few small creatures by giving
Some food that gives them a lift.

If we give just one crumb of food to a bird
And our action comes from pure compassion,
The merit we receive is far greater
Than, from pride, giving something of fashion.

You can practice giving a gift most profound—
Giving your body in four different modes.
You can give, keep, and purify it and
Increase the chance for a human abode.

The greatest tangible gifts we know are
Offerings of what seems most dear.
The most magnificent grants of this kind
Give a life, in aid, without fear.

But we also paradoxically give
When it looks like, rather, we keep.
A life, preserved, in service to others
Comes from love that is pure and deep.

This human body we have
Can take us to the farther shore.
So preserving it for the sake of all others
Brings the spiritual gift adored.

If we preserve our body in this way,
It does not come from cherishing self.
We are using our body in service to others,
And with it, we bring them true wealth.

The body, speech, and mind of a Buddha
Liberate every conscious thing.
Protect and perfect your own three doors;
Shelter from woe, to all, you bring.

We practice purifying our bodies
When we use them in the right way.
Engage only in virtuous acts.
Then vice cannot ever hold sway.

We need to increase the causes for
A fully endowed human revival.
If our goal is not reached in this life,
We are prepared for our new arrival.

The perfection of Giving is present
When we first form the intention to buy.
Preparation to give is always part of the gift—
A form of love upon which all rely.

So purifying and increasing
With the goal to use our body for all
Are gifts no less than things,
And these intangible gifts are not small.

A more propitious type of gift we can give:
Dharma teachings truly spoken.
Material things bring temporary aid;
Dharma renders aid unbroken.

There are myriad ways to give Dharma to others.
We can whisper mantras in ears.
Even our pets can advance from this practice;
This benefit lasts for countless years.

Just one verse of Dharma imparted
Has a value that far exceeds
Magnificent gifts material and all
Other types of virtuous deed.

Give Dharma with the aim to help,
Not for riches or fame.
If these come to you none-the-less,
Winning them has no blame.

Lastly—but with great importance—
Is giving freedom from fear.
Protect from danger and shelter from dread
All others both far and near.

Rescue others from natural disasters:
Floods, earthquakes, and conflagrations.
If unable to directly preserve,
Give your prayers and oblations.

The ultimate source of all our fears
Is the delusion of self-grasping.
Pray for all to be released from illusion;
Act to give relief everlasting.

When Bodhisattvas, from experience, know,
Giving results in reaping great fruit.
With a joyful mind, they've abandoned meanness.
Gladly they give; others follow suit.

Chapter 4

The Engaging Bodhichitta of Patience

Patience is a state of mind
Able to bear pain and abuse.
With Patience, we'll always have peace of mind,
So anger will be of no use.

This perfection shields us from the foe, ire—
The most potent cause of the vices.
It's quite obvious when we see umbrage at work
The suff'ring that, from it, arises.

Anger functions in only one way—
It causes us spiritual harm.
When we injure others in anger,
Our own future wounds are farmed.

Anger can only cloud the mind;
It always leads to deluded view.
Its object appears repulsive;
Equanimity, rather, is true.

As a mind of anger cannot judge truly,
Ev'ry form of Wisdom eludes our view.
Anger always distorts our actions;
Because of this, we have feelings of rue.

When overcome with anger,
We act in regrettable ways.
We separate ourselves from others,
To whom, then, we cannot give aid.

What has caused all wars
And their numberless fatalities?
Angry minds are the root of this scourge
That ravages our commonality.

Anger can make us reject or insult
The belov'd who are our parents.
It can drive us to kill all those we love
And make us take our own presence.

Anger is a blazing fire.
It consumes our minds' virtuous seeds.
As soon as the fire is kindled,
Douse the flames; it is a noble deed.

Those who usually are attracted to us
Are repelled when we're irritated.
When our mind is confused by this terrible flame,
The beauty we have is depleted.

The deceiver, anger, will not help us.
It causes only impairment.
We must subdue this traitor force
To bring ev'ryone betterment.

There is no external enemy
Who harms like this internal bandit.
Others can hurt us in just this one life.
Anger scathes us in all our orbits.

Employ a defense against this Judas, rage;
Strive to keep it at bay.
Meditate on love and compassion,
And you can drive it away.

I, myself, create the conditions of
All my feelings of woe.
It's not a sling or an arrow of outrageous fortune
That is really my foe.

Nothing upsets your mind when you're patient;
You don't ever have complications.
You are no longer vulnerable to
Anxiety, disquiet, frustration.

Patience pertains to three situations.
Keep them in mind; strive to apply.
Endure your distress; Patiently ponder dharma;
Do not take an eye for an eye.

We most proficiently cope with distress,
Accepting it Patiently.
This actually reduces the woe we feel
With anger, increasingly.

Foolishly, we can be cranky when lacking
Mundane pleasures and wealth.
This devious thief only deprives us
Of our spiritual health.

Wealth and poverty are impermanent;
Each brings its own form of pain.
Apply Patience to redirect your mind;
Relieve it of all its strain.

When we have a good reason, we admit our own suff'ring:
Immunizations do not seem so bad.
If we think of the needle as really a help,
Then the suff'ring does not make us feel sad.

When we patiently endure our distress,
We obviate discouragement.
Patience and Effort, with zest, see suff'ring
As a spur to development.

The Patience of enduring suffering
Always employs three virtuous reactions.
You can use it wisely to model and teach
Wisdom, Renunciation, and Compassion.

The act of transforming the suffering we feel
Into renunciation and compassion
Is the heart of the perfection of Patience.
Strive with your Effort to make this your fashion.

When in pain I know I want to progress,
There's no point in feeling frustration.
I have put myself into this spot by past actions.
This brings to mind renunciation.

Rather than feeling self-pity,
Recall the pains and frustrations of all.
Let the thoughts give rise to universal compassion;
One's own pains, then, will begin to look small.

If my suff'ring were to be seen as egregious,
I'd loathe my terrible fate.
But compared to the miseries of my sentient kin,
How fortunate is my state.

If we bear our distress with Patience,
We can harvest a great reward.
Instead of remaining trapped in our pain,
We can find the Wisdom sword.

If pain helps us find this Wisdom sword,
All others can then be helped.
So bring to mind your great compassion, and
Your pain no longer is felt.

Problems and pains are each a danger,
But more so opportunity.
When you encounter these foes, turn them into your friends,
And then smile at them Patiently.

Patiently ponder the teachings of Dharma;
With Effort you will do this with pleasure.
Cultivate this happy mind as you engage in your study;
The result will be growth in full measure.

Steady, calm, joyful endeavor makes our
Practice become like the waxing moon.
With Patience and Effort, we can understand Dharma,
And our Wisdom will come to full bloom.

Although some have said, "Take an eye for an eye,"
Buddha taught something quite other.
Turn your cheek; subdue the flames of anger.
With Patience, the fire you'll smother.

With Patience, you can easily bear
Troubles and indispositions.
When others pain you, bestow gifts of love,
And your power to help sees progression.

We grasp our world and all who harm us
As if they were solid and fixed.
These ideas are only delusions;
Take them out of your mental mix.

The friends, enemies, and strangers we see
Are mentally created congeries.
Empty these biased collections;
A benefactor to all you must be.

Don't foolishly burn your bridges;
Be a trestle for all humankind.
Use compassion to show all sentient beings
How to protect and defend their minds.

If we treat outside foes patiently,
We may win them as friends,
But when treating anger with forbearance,
From worse to worst it tends.

Enduring transgressions with Patience
Is like other pains we admit.
For the greater benefit of our health,
Hurtful treatments we do permit.

View those who harm you as benefactors;
They give you a gift: the chance to practice.
Perhaps they truly may be a Buddha
And appear for your ontogenesis.

When someone clouts us to harm us,
We do not blame the fist that strikes.
The blow results from non-free causes of both
The strike and the striker alike.

A psychiatrist treating mental illness
Views an unruly patient with sympathy.
The cause of wrong action comes from the illness;
Those who harm you, the same you must see.

Someone who harms you is like
A person temporarily insane.
Accept all who maltreat you as clients;
With skill and compassion, heal all their pain.

A mother of a troubled child
Retains her feelings of love, for sure.
Her only hope is for the child's recovery,
And she seeks only that which will cure.

A person who wounds us with words
Cannot harm our body or mind.
It's our anger, itself, that causes us harm.
Strive with Effort, Patience, to find.

Rather than reacting with anger to
One who wants to harm us bodily,
Try to skillfully overcome the problem;
The love you feel, this person may see.

Wanting to preserve the joy of Effort,
The woe of anger I must eschew.
There's no true joy in retaliation;
This is something I must not do.

To practice the Patience of not retaliating,
Recollect two types of karmic fact.
Recall the dangers of succumbing to anger and the
Benefits, without Patience, you'll lack.

Mindful of the karmic facts,
Apply antidote methods that work.
Determine the methods effective for you;
From correct actions you will not shirk.

Having adopted the ultimate goal to
Become a Buddha for all,
All of your actions must serve this purpose;
From that lofty perch, don't fall!

An athlete, in anger, who's tossed from the game
Controverts her final aim.
If a Bodhisattva loses Patience,
He's really doing the same.

Each morning, instruct the guards of your thoughts,
"Be ever mindful and always alert.
If anger transpires within your ken,
Its conquest of my heart you must avert."

We want all Buddhas to notice us
And view us pleasantly.
Their blessings are most assuredly earned
When we act Patiently.

Chapter 5

The Engaging Bodhichitta of Moral Discipline

Moral Discipline is the perfection which aims
To renounce every Bodhisattva flaw.
It's a mental decision—this to do, or a mind which
Blocks a verbal or bodily faux pas.

A seed of non-virtue may ripen
As a fancy to commit a vice.
Refrain deliberately knowing its dangers;
Moral Discipline begins to arise.

Our mind first puts into motion a vice
By contemplating a foolish aim.
Carefully scrutinize each step you consider:
Is it found on the path without blame?

Moral Discipline shields us from
Troubling agitation.
It stops the dangerous invasion
Of the foe contrition.

Moral Discipline is indispensable;
It's prerequisite for a mind at rest.
This perfection is the foundation for
The Concentration all Buddhas have blest.

There are three forms of this perfection.
The first is a kind of restraining.
A second gathers virtuous dharmas; the third
Aims to benefit living beings.

The tethering kind of this superiority is
The Moral Discipline of restraint.
Abstain from non-virtuous thoughts and deeds
And the words that our ignorance taints.

In order to practice this type of control,
We need the faults of non-virtue to know.
We also must make vows to quit the vices and
Fidelity to these promises, show.

The sages have spoken of ten non-virtues
Of particular saliency.
Each of these has three types of effect.
Aware of all of these you must be.

The ten non-virtues also come in three kinds;
The first of these are bodily.
The second are vices of speech,
And those of mind round out the three.

The virtues of body to cultivate
Are to refrain from killing your true kin,
Eschew stealing goods of any kind,
And to sexual misdeeds, don't give in.

Don't lie or engage in divisive speech;
Don't babble words of idle chatter.
Avoid at all times speech intended to hurt.
Ev'ry word you utter does matter.

Our minds must not covet what belongs to another.
Malicious thoughts we must eschew.
Always acknowledge the truths of Dharma;
To reject them is called "wrong view."

The first of the three effects of non-virtue
Is the ripened end of each.
This result is a type of rebirth;
About these, all Buddhas teach.

There are two sub-types of the second causatum;
Both are similar effects to the cause.
These are tendencies to persist in like acts
And encounters similar to the flaws.

The third form of result is environmental
In a human metempsychosis.
Our surroundings may be hostile, threatening,
Or extremely incommodious.

Recall renunciation and compassion;
Reflect on the lives that result
From vicious deeds of yourself and others.
Help all to refrain from faults.

Since what we perceive depends upon
The workings of mind by its own nature,
We can understand how rebirth occurs in hell for
Those who have been a most vicious creature.

We know that Buddha always spoke for our benefit.
He testified, "There are places of torment."
Surely his aim was to tell what's obtained
By minds allowing great vices to foment.

Those who insist the believer in hell
Bears the burden of authentication
Implicitly assume a place of abode
Must be found with our direct perception.

The assumption they have is mistaken;
Though vehemently upon it they insist.
Many entities, we infer, even though in this life,
We never directly see these objects subsist.

From what we give, we eventually get.
Most accept this karmic truth without fail.
There are hells in this world that many observe;
There are those tormented, burned, and impaled.

What we observe in our dreams may have been or will be;
What we dream has a much deeper meaning.
The nightmares of horror that do occur show
What in the future we may be seeing.

Our dreams truly come from the character of our mind;
Awake, it is the same, please know well.
The objects we see are made psychically.
Don't let ignorance make you see hell.

There are hot hells in which the surroundings
Are pervaded by blazing fire.
Because of karmic seeds that ripened at death,
Those there did not take rebirth higher.

We are born in a hell and therein reside until the
Karma that plagues us is exhausted.
In one, we revive over and over, and
We are horrific'ly accosted.

In "reviving hell," we endure
A world of terrifying beings to dread.
Therein, ghastly weapons spontaneously appear.
They pierce us, tear us, and cut us to shreds.

When our life comes to end in reviving hell,
Commanding voices tell us to arise.
We are born again and again in this terrible place,
And we scream and beg to be not alive.

In "black line hell" wherein we encounter
Merciless, brutal, execrable torture,
We are forced to lie down on iron, burning ground,
Our bodies stretched thin like pieces of paper.

Our thin-stretched bodies, in black line hell,
Are branded crisscross with angry, black dashes.
Our tormentors then use the lines as templates
And dice us along them with knives and axes.

In "massed destruction hell," we discover
Animals like we have killed in days of yore.
Their heads appear on huge iron mountains.
We are crushed by these peaks; imagine the gore.

In this same hell, at other times,
It rains boulders galore.
This crushing hail reduces our bodies
To paste and nothing more.

Also in massed destruction hell,
Red-hot rollers may render our bodies oblate
Or huge, burning iron presses
Make a mass of scorched and burning pulp—our poor fate.

In "wailing hell," pitiable beings
Are driven by fear and run to find a safe place.
Finding false shelter in a house made of iron,
It promptly bursts into flames; there is no escape.

As their bodies are incinerated,
They howl and wail in agony.
Although all of this is surreal,
It sadly is no fantasy.

In "loud wailing hell," the screams are stentorian,
And the pains are much more profound.
Our nativity occurs in boiling oil;
Grotesque torturers continuously push us down.

The agonizers use razor-like weapons and
Spears, us to submerge.
They maliciously smash us with clubs
As we reemerge.

In "hot hell," the lamentable beings
Are fried like a fish on red-hot metal.
They are made into skewers, like pieces of meat
And burnt to a crisp, flaming in total.

In the "intensely hot hell," our beloved kin
Are impaled on long, flaming tridents,
And when red-hot metal encases their bodies,
Into molten copper they're then sent.

When the molten copper their flesh removes,
Their skeletons are placed on blazing ground.
Then their flesh grows again to renew their agony;
Back to the boiling cauldrons they're bound.

In the "unceasing torment hell,"
The most horrific hell of all,
The pain begins with a rain of fire
That falls in the form of huge balls.

Then every tissue of the bodies of our kith
Explodes into terrible flames.
Eventually, they resemble only huge bonfires;
Agonizing screams express their bane.

There are neighboring and resembling hells, too;
And for some, a cold hell awaits.
Know the calamity of all these hell beings,
And then upon them meditate.

The neighboring hells include the "pit of fiery ash"
And also the "swamp of excrement."
In one is found only a "plane of sharp razors."
These are, for many, their tenement.

The resembling ordeals occur in this life:
An experience that resembles a hell.
We can hideously burn in a fiery air cash,
Freeze, or be crushed in an earthquake, as well.

Cold hells, with ground incased in thick sleet,
Are surrounded by towering mountains of ice.
The sky is pitch black; a blizzard constantly blows;
The inhabitants: naked because of their vice.

Those who abide in this piceous place
Have bodies that turn cobalt and instantly shrivel.
Hideous blisters form on their frigid skin;
The blisters burst, becoming oozing, ugly pustules.

In this touching state, they wail and moan;
While sneezing mightily, they utter, *"Achoo!"*
In the end, their bodies become brittle and shatter;
At that time, for them, there is naught we can do.

Feel the agony of all these piteous siblings;
Their rescues you must never forsake.
With Generosity, you must model and teach
The virtue that blocks grievous mistakes.

Animals and hungry ghosts also
Your example and lessons are due.
All beings trapped in the pains of Samsara
Must receive Dharma blessings from you.

Your intentions, at all times, from vicious ones block.
Your behavior can then be a standard.
You will model the Moral Discipline of restraint;
To your sentient kin, be a lanyard!

The "Moral Discipline of gathering virtuous dharmas"
Forms the inculpable intention.
The Effort of the same name sees these aims with pleasure.
Now motivation becomes action.

We gather the virtuous dharmas of moral discipline
Through intending the six-fold perfections.
We also should employ a virtuous ten:
The precious, noteworthy Dharma actions.

All ten commissions pertain to missives:
The profound detected in the Dharma.
Write them, read them, and memorize them, too.
These actions constitute good karma.

Recite words of Dharma; to them, make an offering.
Give books and explain what they tell you to do.
Listen to Dharma; contemplate its messages.
Meditate on the convictions that ensue.

The last form of Moral Discipline—
That of "benefiting every conscious thing"—
Is intending to help others in each way we can,
So Buddahood to all we eventually bring.

A sage has taught there are eleven main ways
Of benefiting all of our sentient connections.
Strive to learn them and know their meanings.
Engage in them often in both action and reflection.

One of these ways alleviates suffering, or
Offers others aid in their labor.
A Bodhisattva who does this kind of deed
Is far more than just a good neighbor.

A further mode of beneficence
Imparts skills unknown to others.
Teach Dharma and other worldly skills, too.
Love and help them as a brother.

Another distinct way to be munificent
Returns a kindness received.
You are doing this not to be gifted; again,
Of this, do not be deceived.

Remove dangers that threaten others
And that which causes dread.
Console those who are stricken with grief.
Give food to those unfed.

Those who suffer from strong delusions,
Such as anger and craving attachments,
Will suffer from many problems.
Help resolve these troubling predicaments.

Always be tactful when attempting beneficence;
Sensitive to views and customs please be.
If you don't offer help in ways they accept,
From their troubles you cannot make them free.

Succor those walking correct spiritual paths;
Praise and encourage their righteous actions.
Benefit those on erroneous byways;
With skill and compassion, change their fashion.

To benefit others, Jesus walked on water.
Buddha passed through walls as if space.
A Bodhisattva with miracle powers
Must use them with finesse and grace.

This Moral Discipline of benefiting others
Can easily be seen as combined
With the perfections of Generosity and Effort—
But so too with all the other kinds.

The perfect actions of a Bodhisattva—
Including those of body, speech, and mind—
Are done for the benefit of all others;
So they all become the generous kind.

Thusly, Moral Discipline corrects imperfections.
Its success you can see with intuition.
When all three types of action are harmonious with the Goal,
Moral Discipline has come to fruition.

Chapter 6

The Engaging Bodhichitta of Concentration

Concentration observes an object of virtue
And remains on it tranquilly.
This virtue has pacified all our distractions;
We're focused single-pointedly.

To achieve single-pointed Concentration, attain
Nine mental abidings of subtleness.
Your body and mind will attain the special bliss
Of physical and mental suppleness.

Upon gaining the dual powers of suppleness,
This perfection you will have obtained.
Then use your Concentration; ponder ultimate Wisdom.
Your end goal you have nearly attained.

In order to spur your determination,
This profound perfection to find,
Ponder its benefits until a yen for it
Arises strongly in your mind.

So as to achieve our own happiness—
More so, for all the forlorn—
It needs be we perceive the deep object of Wisdom.
Tranquil mind this must perform.

We can never see an abstruse object
With a mind distracted and wild.
Concentration will subdue the mind's commotion.
You'll become very calm and mild.

Our inborn, untamed, agitated mind
Has discomforts which always attend.
It causes both mental and carnal wounds
Which Concentration can truly mend.

With a peaceful, calm, concentrated mind,
We can always beget virtuous thoughts.
Untarnished thoughts and feelings thereby begotten
Cause the happiness for which we have fought.

To a mind of Concentration come
Wondrous powers in profusion.
A Bodhisattva uses these new-found gifts
To cure *all* of their confusion.

No living presence wants to have faults,
But only Buddhas have attained full perfection.
Concentration is the portal to the room of the Wise.
Open it; become part of this aggregation.

When the ambition to attain Concentration
Is clearly discovered in your perception,
Become a close acquaintance of it;
Repeatedly do placement meditation.

Each day your intention is thereby strengthened,
You will seek Concentration most assiduously
And strive to prepare six essential conditions
That enable development of Tranquility.

The first of the six basal essentials is
A suitable place for retreat.
In this place, you must easily find
Food, clothing, and shoes for your feet.

Your abode should be blessed by Buddhas
And by highly realized beings,
Or our Spiritual Guide may have paid a call.
These events give this place great meaning.

The environment there must also be fit.
Thus the climate temperate should be.
Clean water and air help assure our haleness;
So discover a place most healthy.

We also should find a locale for our practice
Near spiritual friends to give us backing.
The venue must surely be quiet.
With noise, our Concentration is lacking.

Number two on our tally of necessitous conditions:
Greatly diminished worldly desires.
These and other intruding distractions
Waste Concentration as if by fire.

Recall the sloth of the worldly moth—
Attracted, as by light, to the blazing world of woe.
Maintain the Effort of "avoiding meaningless distractions,"
Then through Concentration, your compassion you can show.

The tertian precondition for attaining Concentration
Is contentment with where we are and what we possess.
If you think your food is not tasty or your abode is vexing,
Recall The True Goal, and these displeasures reassess.

The fourth of the six necessitations to assure
Is avoidance of distracting diversions.
When you go on retreat this perfection to seek,
Never spend time on non-Dharma attractions.

The quinary must that underpins our success
Is maintaining pure Moral Discipline.
Tell the guards of your mind to be very vigilant.
The vices at this time must never win.

The endwise member of our six-fold tabulation
Is to occlude distracting conceptions.
Don't think about your doings of the past
Or future worldly plans and projections.

Having assured the essential conditions,
Decide what virtuous objects to observe.
Many before you have traveled this path;
A visualized Buddha has, for them, well served.

If we fix the mind on the form of a Buddha,
Powerful results will then ensue.
We plant virtuous seeds, acquire merit, and
Purify negativities, too.

A Bodhisattva may still have strong delusions
And seek Concentration to counter them all.
Know the opponent mind to a potent confusion;
Abiding tranquilly on it ends the flaw.

Buddha has told us of the three groups of six:
The sense powers, their objects, and minds.
Examine these elements, their parts, and connections;
All are phenomena, you will find.

The most profound phenomenal object is
The non-inherent existence of all.
Bring your mind to rest on interdependence;
The curtain of delusion will then fall.

Renew your Effort when beginning each session,
Feel joy engaging this perfection.
Each step of progression along the path
Will add to your merit collection.

The direct opponent to your aim
Is the obstacle forgetfulness.
You must carefully guard your hold on the object
By the sober watch of mindfulness.

Two further obstacles help define each step
Of progress toward Concentration's great goal.
Mental sinking and excitement wreck our attention
Like a ship running aground on a shoal.

Mental excitement diverts our attention
To distracting objects we like to fancy.
When subtle, only part of our mind will wander;
When gross, this object totally entrances.

Mental sinking reduces our clarity as we
Try to keep our object in mind.
When subtle, the object is clouded by dullness.
When gross, it is gone, you will find.

To attain the perfection of Concentration,
Turn your mind to the object you chose.
Gain in strict order of progression
Nine altitudes of mental repose.

Begin each session, as close as you can,
In Vajrasattva's seven-point posture.
Generate Bodhichitta and form the intention
To gain Concentration for all others.

Begin by achieving a brief repose
At the first stage called "placing the mind."
You're able to keep your object only briefly in view;
You'll lose it and again have it to find.

In "placing the mind," you'll find your distractions
Outnumber the moments of mental repose.
But return after each and every distraction
To the virtuous object of thought you chose.

Meditate repeatedly on the same object chosen;
Your mind becomes somewhat gathered and clear.
When the time you can view it approaches five minutes,
The step "continual placement" is near.

In these first two stages, when you lose the object,
Return to analysis once again.
What are its features or why is it true?
With the answer, you'll afresh find your friend.

With mounting experience in "continual placement,"
A new power anon comes to be.
When regaining focus bereft of analysis,
Your object in "replacement" you see.

When gross excitement and sinking
Have been banished from our immersion,
Although it does waver and is slightly clouded,
"Close placement" is our new attention.

With the total expulsion of all excitement,
When only subtle sinking remains,
The step of "controlling" has arrived,
And alertly we clean each new stain.

But over-applying the antidote, alertness,
In "controlling" to remove sinking clouds
Can reopen the gate to an erstwhile banished enemy.
Slight excitement can oft times be aroused.

When alertness is, in this way, slightly edgy
In watching for sinking's murk,
"Pacifying" is our stage of Concentration.
Finding balance is our new work.

When you learn to balance applying and non-applying
Alertness and mindfulness as focus guards,
Subtle excitement and sinking will pose little danger.
"Completely pacifying" is now in charge.

In the "completely pacifying" Concentration,
When subtle excitement or sinking faze,
Our Effort will recognize the displeasure
And back to joyous focus move our gaze.

At the penultimate level, "single-pointedness"
No longer distractions or clouding manifest.
To maintain our Concentration, we still must sometimes
Make mental exertions to maintain our mind's rest.

"Placement in equipoise" is the ninth and last level.
Reaching this is most blest.
After exertion to bring the mind to our object,
It with ease stays at rest.

Perfect Concentration will at last develop
After equipoise in placement.
The suppleness induced by this abiding
Is Concentration's attainment.

Slight suppleness can first be perceived
On the second level of focus.
But complete suppleness is attained after
Reaching the ninth and final locus.

This suppleness, to some, appears quickly.
But others must meditate for weeks
In placement in equipoise
Before this dear attainment is reached.

With the suppleness found in Concentration,
We finally are free
From the stiffness of all our mental and physical
Inflexibility.

With suppleness, our mind becomes clear.
Obstacles to virtuous actions are gone.
Physical suppleness comes from the mental;
Our body is quite tireless and strong.

These flexibilities have come
From supple energy flows.
The energies within have become quite ductile;
With bliss, our body now glows.

From the bliss of physical suppleness
That of mind quickly will arise.
A bliss that first quivered from shock
Becomes stable before our eyes.

This new-found, stable bliss, so named
The "unchangeable bliss of captivation,"
Is the sure and noble sign of
Reaching the perfection of Concentration.

Our phenomenal experience now is
As if we have dissolved into the object.
Our mind has become completely clear,
As though counting atoms could be our project.

Our mind no longer is attached
To any realm of desire.
We can nevermore take lower rebirth
But only to those much higher.

Now Concentration can bear its full fruits.
We gain higher spiritual grounds and paths.
Turn your mind to focus on Wisdom,
And you will become a Buddha at last.

Chapter 7

The Engaging Bodhichitta of Wisdom

The essence of the Perfection of Wisdom
Is known as Superior Seeing.
In Concentration, examine your object.
Then find the suppleness of learning.

The suppleness of learning arises
From repeated, concentrated clear-viewing.
Acquire superior insight into your object's true nature.
Supple knowing is Superior Seeing.

We can't infer or discover self-existent objects.
We've projected them from beginningless time.
In grasping the pleasers and rejecting the teasers,
Our own foolishness is the most vicious crime.

Every object we observe is truly empty
Of something with which we ignorantly perceive it is filled.
We think they're chock full of self-existence and
Want them in our control.
This grasping and pushing is why we're continually killed.

Emptiness of self-existence
Has a sibling that is its twin.
Dependent Arising has the same Mother.
Know Her your Buddhahood to win.

Sage Nagarjuna prostrated before Buddha,
Giving praises to this best of teachers.
He thanked him for giving four pair-wise cogitations
And no description of this strange creature.

"Unceasing, unborn," he said Buddha taught
Is the child, Dependent Origination.
So speaking, Buddha meant this way of existing
Is the only meaningful explanation.

Unannihilated yet not permanent?
This must be the Middle Way!
Neither thinking things are permanent nor else wise, there is nothing
Should e'er o'er our mind hold sway.

"Not coming, not going,"
Not here or there, not now and even not then?
There is no unique space-time event way
Of finding anything we want to befriend.

"Without distinction, without identity."
We can't find it within nor distinguish it from without?
What is the point of all this negativity?
Liberation for ev'ryone is what it's all about.

The "Free from conceptual construction" teaching,
Which Nagarjuna thanks Buddha for,
Schooled us we can never describe the Suchness
We will find when on the farther shore.

A self-identical thing can't be found here-now nor there-then
And also neither without nor within;
We won't find it no matter where-when or how we look.
So let this strangely thorough search begin.

Oft times when we are negating,
We affirm with the not-words we have spoken.
If I'm "not late," I'm either "early" or "on time."
To find Emptiness, this practice is broken.

When you investigate the question,
"Can one find a unicorn?"
You don't find a thing called non-unicorness;
Rather, existence is shorn.

So *Emptiness* is a mere name;
To no object can it refer.
It's rather the absence of something
We suppose does really occur.

We think that what we normally see
Are objects free from mental creation.
But the conclusion we will seek to show true is
More radical than Kant's cogitations.

Things we observe are made by the mind,
And we do not mean only a few.
But no mental substance is making these objects.
Be more radical than Berkeley, too!

"If everything is empty," you may joke,
"Is Emptiness empty, too?"
Although to some, this may at first sound funny,
This thought we do not eschew.

We begin by adopting two forms of truth;
A simple account simply cannot be true.
Some truths must be called conventional;
Correspondence with the way things are won't do.

Conventional truths accord with our talk;
"That is a snake" is true when it impeccably acts.
We can experience a snake when "It's really a rope"
Is what is actually, by convention, a fact.

This seeing a rope as a snake
Is what imputation by mind can bring.
Mind forms an object upon the basis
Of a collection of some other things.

A statement is ultimately true
When it asserts what's true about the way things are.
But prior to reaching enlightenment,
You can't espy this truth anywhere near or far.

But don't stop at mere enlightenment;
Obstructions to full cognition remain.
Don't forget you're aiming to reach full Buddhahood,
And all others you want to do the same.

We have to learn this ultimate truth
Through reliance upon clear analytic-thinking.
So we reason not for the fun of contradicting others, but
To bring a conclusion to highest Concentrating.

We begin by reviewing distinctions
That can serve us ably for many a purpose.
There is physical stuff and mental stuff, too;
As conventional credo, they can well aid us.

There is me and everything other;
Some things are mine, and some we think are not.
There are conscious things, and some do not observe,
And into Emptiness falls this whole lot.

A division of conscious perceivers is known
Only by the accomplished few.
A small child from on high thinks people are the size of ants;
Their minds cannot grasp point of view.

If you've ever watched a nature TV show
With a cat sitting close to your knee,
You'll know that a cat thinks a bird on the screen
Is the same as a bird in a tree.

We wizened, adult human beings all know
The cat's only confused by the image she sees.
We know that the bird on the screen is different
From a "real" cat in whose existence we believe.

Some know we always see a phenomenal bird,
But they say we should have faith that there is one out there.
These wise humans tell all the others,
"You're much like that cat as you sit smugly in your chair."

These relatively sage humans have told us,
"Be content with these objects of mind.
It really doesn't make much difference to pine;
Knowledge of them is all you can find."

Such sages deny this knowledge is conventional,
Saying, "It's universal reason at work.
I assure you, the mind functions in only this way."
This is one of their intellectual quirks.

I heard a knock upon my door one evening
While sitting there feeling smug in my chair.
Let's go to see who could be there, I thought;
It's a young lady who has a blank stare.

This sad, suffering child in confusion
Said she recently came to a profound conclusion.
"I think I once was Immanuel Kant
'Cause of memories that have come in profusion.

"Now, I don't know where my mom or my dad is;
This makes me so very sad.
Please take me in and explain my confusion.
Then I might not feel so bad."

"Yes, please do enter, my dear, and tell me what you are called."
"I don't know," she said. So then said I, "Immanuella,
I'd like to choose."
Some confusion cleared from her eyes while saying,
"I have an inkling it's really all the same no matter
The name you use."

"Well then, Ella, please take a chair;
If you'd like, please pet my cat."
"That pussy will not make me feel any better."
She pouted from where she sat.

I thought this over for just one moment before,
"To a movie," I said, "Let us go."
She said, "I only have the vaguest memories
Of seeing this persuasion of show."

I said, "A movie tells a story of people and other things
By moving pictures projected onto a screen."
"What's a movie, in itself," pondered Immanuella,
"If it's just a light-made representation scene?

"Such a thing is really quite odd," she burst out,
"Representing representations of things I hope are out there."
I, by now a bit tweaked by her pique, thought,
"A 3D movie with flying balls would really give her a scare."

Luckily, *Tennis, the Movie* in 3D was playing across the street.
With Ella's hand in mine and feeling a good bit of cheer,
Across the street we safely went while I was thinking,
This will be fun for me, and Ella can learn from her tears.

I jovially bought our tickets and then
I quickly scouted for free chairs.
Ads and previews filled our view;
At the screen she intently stared.

We took the seats that I had found,
And then the show began.
It panned over the court below,
Then high at the people in stands.

Back to a powerful woman
In red tennis apparel
The scene then shifted.
Her strong arms were a marvel.

High above her head, she lifted both of her arms,
About to deliver her serve.
The ball careened off her racquet;
Directly toward our heads it swerved.

Ella screamed in terror, and then
Jumping completely out of her blue chair,
She ran toward the exit, still shrieking.
She wanted to be anywhere but there.

With as much composure as I could muster,
Out of the theater, her, I followed.
But being a compassionate person,
A lump in my throat I had to swallow.

I had to run as fast as I can
In order to catch the young girl.
In about thirty seconds, I caught hold of her hand
As a cold wind howled and swirled.

I quickly took her back across the street,
Then into my clement apartment.
I knew the young girl needed this lesson, but
I felt bad about my deportment.

Ella still had enormous eyes,
And her fright nearly made her swoon.
I gave her a glass of water
And hoped we could discuss this soon.

It seemed an almost interminable time
Before Ella had recovered.
"This experience really made me feel," she spoke,
"As if I was being smothered."

It had taken about thirty minutes to calm her;
She eventually did pet my cat.
I then strolled across the room to my easy chair.
We began to talk from where each sat.

"Ella, the spheroid that seemed ready to hit your head
Was not what we can really call a tennis ball.
It had the appearance of being one,
But its functioning wasn't like one much at all.

"The balls that you know and thought you saw
Can be held by you in your hand.
I hope that what I plan to tell you
Is something you can understand."

Ella replied that, "What I saw
Had been held by what a person who has helped has lent.
So what I think, therefore, I saw function was what I have
Formerly seen as a regular type of event.

"The fright was really tremendous, because
The ball was coming right at my head;
The ball then went right through my noggin,
And I thought I must surely be dead.

"Either death could be my fate, I thought,
Or I hoped it was a just bad dream.
Because instantly I had the first reaction,
I felt that I really must scream."

"Ella, what you saw, my dear,
Was for you a completely new type of event.
A ball of computer and mind creation definitely
Has no in itself ball from which it was sent.

"In order for you to see this event,
The conditions from which it arose needn't include a ball at all.
If the writer and director had intended,
A beach ball from the screen is what you would have said you saw.

"The appearances you saw in the movie
Do have a causal explanation.
But it is similar in many ways to those you call dreams and other
Things of idle imagination.

"I read you wanted to avoid
What you thought would be a terrible tragedy
In finding morality a thing of idle imagination,
And you said you found autonomous equity.

"In grounding morality in a new kind of
Causality you think you have found,
You now have not just one category of
Causation you think is profound.

"This doubling of causation could begin
A serious problem, I think.
It may, Ella, be something you should
Consider as something to shrink."

"I really think I'm much too tired
To consider this problem right now.
Please, may I prepare for bed?
But I hope I can fix it somehow."

"Yes, young lady, it really is late;
The sun has completed its diurnal course.
Tomorrow will bring new adventures;
Let us hope that your problems don't get much worse.

"Tomorrow I think I will sleep late.
And later, some important thinkers will meet us.
I think you may benefit from a different moral look, so
If bored, please look at Shantideva's fine treatise.

"It explains the path of the Sons and Daughters of Buddha—
Those with universal love.
They aim to eliminate all sentient beings' suffering by
Advancing to a state above.

"Rule following. Some rules, you say, display freedom, but others are
Duties; imperfect, you call them, and you then hold
Them with kid gloves,
Because they attend to love, which you say enslaves.
The Children strive for perfections that come in the
Shape of true love."

"I'll consider it," said Ella as she wobbled off to bed so as
To find some respite in her sleep from her feelings of dread.
I myself pondered what she might hear tomorrow,
But as for tonight, I reflected, no more should be said.

In the morrow, I awoke quite late because of
Exhaustion from searching for truth.
Ella said, "I had time to read your book."
I asked, "You read the book, forsooth?"

"My dear guardian, Shantideva's book is quite sentimental
And shows a lack of correct understanding
Of the sources of all factual duties.
When he learns what's what, he'll have a hard landing."

I said, "Someone, I'm sure, will hit the canvas
When our search for truth is done.
Although I wish for no one to suffer,
I'm sure all this will be fun.

"Have you eaten anything since you arose,
My delightful young female friend?
Because if you're full and ready to go,
To new business we must attend."

"What have you in mind, my
Patron, during the time I can't find my loyal mother?"
I said, "My dear, have no fear;
Since you learned from yesterday's show, let's go to another."

"I'm stronger now than in bygone times, she said,
So the fear that gripped me before
When confronting day dreams, which are new to me,
Will not trouble me anymore."

"Okay let's go again; this time I've invited Richard and Annette.
We all will join Erwin there and the Mother
None of us knows.
I phoned her once to ask from whence she came and heard this in reply,
'Everywhere and nowhere, too, but, from your East,
You can suppose.'

"Can you briefly describe yourself," said I,
"So when I try to find you I can?
She said, 'My mind is empty with bliss,
And my form appears with just four hands.'"

Mother should be pretty easy to pick out of a crowd, I thought.
As Ella and I strolled up to the theater, we quickly
Found my friend, Annette.
I was about to introduce them to each other, but Annette said,
"Hello. Ella, please call me Dr. Annette Mrs. Kurt Baier,
As we have just met.

"I can't be identified separately from my history.
I am a thread in the fabric of my relationships.
Eventually, you'll need to learn the other connections I have.
Kantian persons are like a captain without a ship."

Annette asked me who else will be joining us.
Replied I, "Richard and Erwin; I think we will have fun.
Another will also appear—the Mother none of us knows.
I also asked Doctor John, but he said he couldn't come.

"He said he was busy packing for a trip to Boston,
Where he would be giving a talk at a school.
He asked what movie I had in mind, and
I told him it's a movie portraying some fools.

I told him we were planning to go and
See *Planet of the Orangutans.*
He said, 'That's just the same old thing
About a theme of which I'm a fan.

"'But since I've seen this story over and over
And explained it in detail,
I don't need to see it again, because I am well aware of
The foolishness it entails.

"'It's really only about the absence of humanity,' he continued,
'That predominates in the pursuit of science.
Having explained this to many in full, I have found now
There's a large pool of people to be my clients.'"

What we had said made Ella's head spin with memories flooding in.
Richard and Erwin appeared, and I found our friend, Mother.
I tried to introduce all of them to Ella, who said,
"Because of what you both told me, I can't see the others."

I then asked a vendor for tickets. Ella said she saw a person of dignity
Fastidiously giving back the right change.
I looked at Erwin, Richard, Annette, and the Mother
And felt that quickly all things would become strange.

This is what happened next. Annette nudged Ella and said,
"My dear, that's just a puffed-up peacock."
Noticing I was agitated from searching for truth, Richard told me,
"Relax, friend. Behold my calm.
Truth depends upon with whom you talk.

"Learn how to fit in, but stay away from objectivists."
The Mother and Erwin winked at each other.
Erwin then asked me if I had brought my cat along in a box, because, he said,
"I've a device for it I've discussed with Mother."

Ella said, "I'm beginning to think I don't know what's happening.
What are persons? What is true?
Annette and Richard have left me wondering,
What in this world should I do?"

The Mother said, "'Ella, dear, what the others have said
Are ideas to which you should attend—
All except Richard's advice to stay away from objectivists.
There are some of them I recommend."

We all then went and took our seats
To watch this interesting show
Which depicted the Earth with mad scientists
Wanting to enhance what apes know.

The star of this fantastic attraction
Was an orange ape that was named Gus.
I guess I really should have said *who* and not *that,*
'Cause he sure thought a lot like us.

A scientist worked for a company chief
Who wanted to make a whole lot of money.
This scientist thought that science should seek to
Find a way to help his dad not look funny

To other people because of his memory loss
Resulting from the dreaded Alzheimer's disease.
The scientist actually had a lot of compassion
For his dad and thus wanted to put him at ease

By helping to eliminate his worry about a future in which he
Would suffer from confusion and failure to know
What was going on in the world around him—who he was
And who his loved ones were. We are all like this, so

This scientist was, in a way, just like the greedy,
Self-centered company chief, because although the scientist
Didn't want people to be harmed by his research,
His circle of concern was limited and thus amiss.

You see, the greedy company chief cared only about himself
And maybe those persons who were
Family and friends,
And the scientist cared about his family and coworkers
And even to some degree about Gus. But that is not
Where this story ends.

As Dr. John attested, this movie was part of a continuing
Story about how people, as a result of their stupidity,
Destroy their way of life in such a way that
Earth comes to be ape-dominated by serendipity.

Dr. John believes that scientists must integrate a
Sense of humanity into their understanding
Of what the purpose of science is. Bodhisattvas
Would accept that his position has some standing,

But using the word *humanity* for the need to
Integrate moral values into what scientists do
Would seem to them to be a term connoting a rather
Limited scope of concern—that is, to the human few.

Something that this movie has in common with
The previous show seen—*Tennis, the Movie* in 3D—
Is the inclusion of computer thing-generation. For apes,
Human beings in costumes is not what you see.

So we all went in and saw this movie and agreed
Post hoc to frequent a coffee shop after a short walk,
Where we would relax, have a latte or two,
And enjoy a very stimulating ev'ning of talk.

We were enjoying our lattes when Ella said,
"I am not really certain what I just saw
In this very unusual movie with talking
And thinking apes killing people, short and tall.

"Is Dr. John right that it is about the lack of humanity
In the pursuit of science? Really, I think greed
Was the problem. Teaching the company chiefs
To respect humankind's dignity is the need.

"And I have another question," she continued.
"Are there really apes that can talk and reason
Like humans now because of the fact that
They got a shot of smart vaccine in the wrong season?

"And I have an observation. Gus certainly became
A powerful and crafty general in his management
Of his ape friends against the baffled and confused
Men not familiar with his military accomplishment."

It was at this moment that I recited my interpretation
Of the moral lesson of this movie show,
And then I continued, "Gus was computer-generated,
So costumed humans were not his friends in tow.

"At this time, you are not very likely to encounter, in this room,
A phenomenal experience that you can confidently describe
As an ape army functioning under the direction of an orangutan
As we did describe the cinematic functioning of Gus and his tribe."

Annette entered the conversation at this point and said to Gus,
"It should have been—but probably was not—obvious
To you that there was not a single lady ape actually identifiable in this
Movie. As usual, men are only screwing us.

"The eventual out-of-control ape rage was
Inevitable in an ape society completely ignoring
The wisdom of women. However,
I know the paucity of your imagination makes this sound boring."

Annette then said, "Ella, another theme you should have
Noticed in this movie was the entire destruction
Of the early personality that was developing as Gus.
He was torn from the fabric of normal maturation.

"The normal construction of a personality takes place partly
Within the context of being the birthed child of a particular
Mother at a particular place and time. Kantian persons are
Unseen in reality, even with magical binoculars.

"Of course, I don't mean to say that the adopted
Child of a mother has necessarily been
Torn out of the fabric of her personality;
However, with older children, this can be seen.

"Kantian persons are supposedly somewhere beyond Kant's aesthetic,
Transcendental realm of space, time, and causality
But in fact are one fictitious person, because they
Are just intuited as abstract mentality.

"Gus can only become a person within the context
Of nurturance both by his mother's caring contentment
And of his knowledge of the moral structure
Formed culturally but reflecting humane sentiment.

"Gus's normal maturation was not destroyed merely
Because he acquired skills heretofore unknown in apes.
Human personalities before have developed in this way.
Technology often gives human behavior new shapes.

"Rather, Gus was torn completely from his context. He
Was in strange ground which he must have experienced as bizarre.
He must have felt totally uprooted, like being a seven-year-old girl
Whisked from ancient Greece into the body of a Russian Czar.

"In this way," Annette continued, "someone can be destroyed and yet
Be born again as the same but much different person.
This is my understanding of part of what you saw.
As a caring person, I give to you this hard lesson."

"Annette, who's stitching the cloth?
There must be some real persons there.
Threads alone can do no knitting," Ella replied.
"Real persons must put them together.

"And these persons can't knit a quilt
In just any which way each other may wish.
The threads must not be treated as objects.
Your persons sit in a phenomenal dish.

"I now realize that the phenomenal quilt my look queer from
Konigsberg; right now, I'm looking away from there.
But we must not let the stitching remain in the
Hands of persons who see the threads as objects mere."

Annette parried, "What you're saying, Ella, are Immanuel's words,
'To protect the threads, see them as noumena, we must.'
But there is a better way of talking about the problem.
Get rid of noumenal persons, and think about trust.

"We don't have to be external to our fabric to weave it.
Threads emerge from within the ground of all things.
We are like dust blown from a dry field; into this field, it resettles.
Know this and all the happiness that it brings.

"In the dusty field of love, there is no need for the
Puffed-up peacock of respect.
We only need to allow each other to settle into this dusty field.
Do this, and feel no regret."

Just then, Richard, Dr. Rorty, interjected, "If one correctly
Understands truth, then one might be trustworthy.
Truth seems to me to unravel from a flaw about your 'truth.'
You say knowledge is about the phenomena that we all see,

"And you claim that when we speak the truth, we
Must first look at the phenomena and see them
As having been structured by the mind's universal
Categories such as substance, causality, and time.

"Then if we apply the methods of science in the use of them,
We shall be as confident as one possibly can be
That what we are saying about the phenomena is true.
More categories—the moral ones—you then claim to see.

"So Immanuel and Ella think that we all must see the same
Things when we properly investigate
The phenomena formed
By the mind using its own universal ways.
But we all can investigate in these ways, and
Truths can still non-conform.

"First, dear Ella, encounter the thoughts of anyone who
Thinks like someone other.
An encounter with group-thinking to you incomprehensible
Can your objects smother.

"Of course, I don't mean those who hear 'Snow is white'
And are speakers who can only say *'Schnee ist weiss'*
Are in group-thinking wholly other, but
There is no universal translating device.

"In encountering deep differences such as seeing a tidal wave
Striking Japan as a stunning display of the wrath of God,
Whereas in different point of view, someone
Claims to have seen only God's loving wherever they have trod,

"We are encountering ways of seeing through strangers' eyes.
Strangers can find these different things.
Their strange but internally consistent views do not violate any rules
Or categories through which you view all your things.

"This applies to both of the views you have adopted:
'Finding and viewing the facts of science through my method'
And 'finding the facts of morality through my method.'
Problems arise between these two groups because of the mud

"Of objective truth into which we all usually fall.
When group-thinkers with vastly diff'rent views
Meet and each group clings to an objective view of truth,
Then clashes and violence can ensue.

"It occurs to me that what is happening is that people whose
Truths are questioned cling tightly to something they are making,
But not Seeing.
Their talk creates both themselves and the things they are shaking

"Before the eyes of the other group so as to scare and intimidate
The other group into seeing their own selves and their own things
The way they think anyone must see them.
Ponder all of the heartbreak and suffering this brings.

"I looked into my own self-making and noticed
That this used to occur, and I suspect you will come
To the same finding, should you look into your self-making.
Let go of objective truth; soothe yourself for fun

"It seems to me that perhaps you derive joy from trying to intimidate
Others into your way of viewing the world by your shallow
Arguments that this is the Way of Seeing. Quiet your troubles; accept
Truth as conventional. Let your categories lay fallow."

At this point, "I" felt as if "I" really had to enter into "this
discussion."

"I" was internally putting all of the noun words into
Scare quotes, because "I" did not want to object to all that
Richard and Annette had said about the
Conventional nature of truth, persons, and objects.

"I" believe that when worldly people use noun words,
They almost always think that these words do refer
To things-in-themselves/things-with-a-self.
Since "I" reject this, "I" (in quotes) all nouns prefer.

"I" accept that all persons, all objects, and all
Truths worldly people observe and accept
Are merely conventional designations.
Most statements using nouns, finally true, "I" reject.

"I," thinking that
The people gathered into our small "groupings"
Needed to observe a particular part of
Attending-understanding-considering, and

"I," believing that in order for the kind of
Attending-understanding-considering
"I" was wanting to arise, "I" would have to become involved,
Because few westerners know this mode of thinking

Or talking.

"I" can appear a bit strange to other people,
Because "I" think that Greek and Latin
Are great languages, for with them, one can
State a sentence with no noun therein.

However, really only a few
Such sentences using only verbs sound right to these ears.
"Raining," they allow, is a sentence that's okay.
What I said above would, as sentences to them, sound quite queer.

"I" suppose that "you" probably think that
Attending-understanding-considering
Is a weird noun, but "I" am now going to make an
Even stranger statement:
"Attending-understanding-considering."

Do "I" seem weird to "you"?
"I" believe the weird statement above is conventionally true
But that ultimately, it is false.
Right now, as you are reading this poem, "I" hope
That statement is true.
Maybe "you" just batted that statement away,
But "I" want all of the "yous" eventually to bat it around.
"I" am now going to jump into the fray and stop using scare quotes.
"You" are probably tired of them anyway.

"Richard, I have no objection at all
To claiming there is just a name-made self.
However, I cannot agree with your claim that all truths are
Conventional. This belief we must shelve.

"In making the claim that all truths are conventional, you assert
What you must admit is a conventional truth. But then you
Must accept that those saying that truth is objective have
As true a claim as your claim that objective truth has no proof.

"How can your concept of truth possibly widely obtain
The result you think is so good?
The believers in objective truth simply reject your claim, some
Saying God tells me what I should

"Take as true, and He tells me there is objective truth.
You can't convince everyone they must give up 'objectively true'
Unless you can convincingly defend the statement,
'My theory that all truth is conventional is objectively true.'

"Good luck.

"People who believe all truths are objective usually cling to their
Truths and often try to kill those
Who offend their selves when you deny their objective truths.
There are two truths we must convince.

"When someone learns that there are ways to know
Both the objective and conventional truths,
The calm feelings and peace that you recommend
Can arise from understanding the two truths."

Said Richard, then, "I regret to say although we've met,
I've never learned you to name.
Please tell me how I should refer to you, and
Then I will name you the same.

"After I adopt a way to direct my words to you,
I'll happily begin to discuss this strange claim.
I assure you I will always remain calm and pleasant;
Please kindly assure me that you'll do the same."

"Richard, my kin, as you know,
I have no true name. As my role in this
Poem is to protect young Ella from harm, just point and say,
'The Guardian.' Me you can't miss.

"I sincerely promise you, Richard,
To no one am I truly a threat.
I have worked quite assiduously to try to
Love everyone I have ever met,

"And everly I will meet."

"Okay, Guardian, I have a challenge or two
To this notion there are two truths.
I assert that truth is a unitary concept, and there
Are only the false and the truth.

"If you split truth into two different kinds,
Then what is to stop finding some more?
This silly ship with two rudders
Is sure to run aground on that shore.

"In computer programming, we only assign the false and
The truth to our sentences.
So you will wreck our one-truth computers. Your two
Truths will cause us menaces."

"Richard, it is simply not true that we have
Only one truth in language.
We do use truth within our object languages and
Also in meta-language.

"Some think that object language true is not one.
Ask Professor Belnap.
More than one object language true he thinks he has found.
One truth is merely crap.

"I agree that in all object languages,
Truth is merely conventional.
But when we move to the meta-level,
A different kind of truth is eventual.

"As for the claim that computer logic requires
Only two values of truth named *true* and *false*
And in programming named *one* and *zero,* I
Will take you to a dance where we both can waltz.

"The conventional plane of experience in
Which we see both subjects and objects
Differs from the ultimate plane, and
These planes do actually intersect.

"The ultimate plane in which no selves
Are found is not a world that's transcendent;
It is not noumenal. It's a way in which we actually see
Objects without existence-inherent.

"By *inherent-existence,* I'm using just words,
And I think we can say that we've come to agreement
That the objects we talk about are merely named,
And there is nothing we might name the self-existent.

"I name this 'the plane of seeing dependent co-arising' or 'Seeing,'
Because on this plane, objects have not disappeared.
If a mind has no content at all and everything has disappeared, then
Nothingness results, which is what Parmenides feared.

"Mind and content are an interdependent coin of two faces,
Not subject and object. A mind
Without any content at all
Is something we never will find.

"And content without mind beholding it
Also can never be found.
Both Ella and I have come to this conclusion
By arguments that are sound.

"Now, numbers also come on two planes—
The imaginary and the real.
But imaginary numbers we know are not silly; they
Have uses that we can see and feel.

"And one of the interesting uses
Of numbers called the imaginary
Is in what is called the processing of signals.
And information contained signals be.

"And of course, statements are, in this very sense, signals,
Because signals are not just containers of information;
Their true worth is in the transmission of information.
Signal processing is the transmission of information.

"Your objection that programming is undermined by adding truth
In the Seeing plane
Is mistaken, because by employing an imaginary number, using it is
Not really a pain.

"Since the imaginary and real number planes
Intersect at the number zero,
Falsehood remains assigned the zero,
But two number ones are our heroes.

"Just as in the eighteenth century when
The imaginary numbers we thought to be flaky,
It may be that this
Unusual theory will at first be seen as shaky.

"In both languages, I do propose,
Truth should come with an adjective.
In object languages, *Conventional,* and in the Meta, *Ultimate,*
The adjectives to truth we give.

"In the logic we use in both arguments and computers,
We should still use the number one and apply
This value to conventional truths. In the ultimate
Plane, the number to use should be one times i.

"In logic, we can still use the capital *T*
But apply it only to truths ultimate.
For conventional truth, I suggest we place
The small letter *t* on our truth-value plate.

"So our truth tables need big *T,* little *t,* and *F.*
Arranging them systematically will be quite neat;
One times i, of course, may
Only be assigned to an ultimate Truth we speak.

"One remains the value assigned to
All conventional truths. Zero still goes to all statements False.
That the intersection of the two kinds occurs at the value of False
Can be seen as what makes the seeming disunity no fault.

"However, one clarification in truth-value saying
About assigning a value to the bi-conditional—
It must be one i for *TT* and one for *tt,* and
When mixing *Tt,* the zero must become traditional.

"When assigning the value of the bi-conditional,
We still can attend to the parts of double arrow.
And we still will see the same number when we
Attend to the conjunction, as it is the marrow

"Of the bone from which the bi-conditional is made.
Look to the truth values of the conjuncts from which
This bone is made. If the value of the conjunction
Is zero, there's no need in this system to switch

"To a different truth value than that.
If the value is one, it still stays the same.
If the value is one i, do not change your course.
If you stick to this plan, you will not be shamed.

"The unity of the number system is not only at zero;
'The imaginary numbers and real ones are separate' is just False.
In just this same way,
'The planes ultimate and conventional are separate' is also False.

"I expect that with the passage of time,
Ingenuity will help us search and find
Other uses that may be handy for our two values of truth,
But we must decree not to mix the two kinds

"Of truth in a chain of argument
In order to block a bad inference
Between the two levels. We must buy for
Us some two-truth insurance.

"Although we can combine in our one-truth logic
French sentences and those spoken in English,
In this case, we are combining just conventional truths,
So mixing them cannot cause us real anguish.

"But since meta-statements are in a different plane,
Mixing the two truths leads to untruth.
All such combined statements
We must ban as being quite uncouth.

"Such mixed-up combinations
May sound as though they make some sense,
But all such statements are just meaningless. They
Are false, because they are nonsense."

Answered Richard, "It seems an interesting theory—
This two-truth theory you propose.
However, I am not convinced.
Don't it on me try to impose.

"For one thing, you will have to convince
Me that there is something true
With a capital *T.*
Saying something True would you behoove."

"You are asking me, Richard, to state
A truth in the meta language
Where I will be talking about
Statements in an object language?"

"Yes, Ella's Guardian, that is
Exactly what I want to hear.
I am not convinced that all true is
Not in the conventional here.

"I still believe it is in the sentences
With which I am addressing you.
I hope you can say something.
I don't want you to be blue."

"All statements S in a rich object language L, such that S states
'There exists an x such that x is P-predicated' are false."
I then said, "I have returned to the English object language.
I-ly Truly spoke.
Bertrand-ly truly has written."

Richard said, "Me-ly about-your-weird-talking-thinking.
It appears we soon quiet meta-talking.
Its one-sentence paucity seems to me problematic, Mr. Guardian, and
I think there's another problem still lurking.

"I accept that only mere names are
Found in what can be called our object languages,
But 'All statements are false in rich object languages'
Seems too extreme. Prove this, if you can manage."

"Not [necessary], Guardian-ly, that to do.
Not Guardian-ly that will be doing.
Tarskily, that has been done."

Richard then said, "Well, I wish you would end
This queer way of talking, but I did understand.
However, I don't recall
Tarski did that. Please help me See. Lend me a hand."

"Richard, you should recall that Tarksi
Showed that any language as rich
As our object languages be is necessarily
Inconsistent. Ain't that a bitch?

"Of course, from an inconsistent set of
Premises, one can prove any statement at all.
So I can prove a lot of things that make us look silly. Because
It is quite true that I can prove 'Large is small.'

"I can prove that at this time, right here in this room,
It is both raining and not raining at all.
I can prove the sun is also the moon.
I can prove there is motion and there is no motion at all.

"I can take Tarksi's proof and call it
'The law that every statement in a rich object
Language is both true and false.' I am so sorry to tell you
That to this law you cannot logically object.

"I have an idea! Let's call it Tarski's Law.
It's sort of like DeMorgan's Law.

"With Tarski's Law, we can show
That with the systems of languages we
Are using, now we get thorough utter inconsistency.
No wonder sage Zeno felt so much glee.

"Worldly beings cannot suddenly stop believing that
Some statements are true, 'cause all of them might fall off a cliff.
However, these foolish, so prideful beings are always
Jumping into the abyss
Of Suffering. I hope when they hear this, they won't be miffed.

"But what I said in the meta-language
Can help to us understand how things really be.
And please note that the paradox of the heaps
Can also be solved by using meta-Big *T.*

"Every part of the heap is not a real heap,
And even among the parts, together, one cannot be found.
We can derive from our Meta-Truth that sand heap does not exist.
To stay on our feet, when worldly, we must use the *t* you found."

"We must agree with Dr. Russell that
The statement 'There is a sand heap' means
There exists an x, such that x is a heap and x is sand.
We've created the existence extreme.

"We each acquire the ability to create
Sand heaps when people teach us how to speak.
But just as the paradox says, we cannot ever add enough
Grains to the pile to make it a real heap.

"Part of what mommy does when she teaches us to
Speak is to utter, 'That's true!'
When we point at a shoe in a children's book
And say 'shoe,' Mommy says, 'Shoe!'

"'Yeaaaaaaaa!'

"This 'true' is in the object language,
And it always stays there,
So we find that Tarski actually with us
Did a good-news paper share.

"Philosophers must tell us and show us
That we only have 'conventional true'
In 'rich object languages' and that to find True, we must
Put it in meta-language and not rue.

"Rotating the unified plane of truth
Is different from how one i we first got.
In the plane of numbers we multiply by i as
To the 'truth one' we multiply by naught.

"'There exists and x, and x is a heap, and 'x is made of sand'
Is true in English whenever we do agree.
But when we move to True in the meta language,
An existing sand heap we never can see.

"Now, in the meta-language, we look at all the
False statements obtained by this process,
And we notice a peculiar fact:
These conventional truths are a mess.

"We notice that the statements are constantly
Growing at incredible speed, adding to true
False. We notice these statements keep getting
Longer because of appending *false* to *true.*

"We see that it was true that the
Sun is shining, and then we see
It is false that it is true that a thing
Called the Sun a shining thing be.

"So is 'The Guarding is talking' really true or false?
As in this infinite processing,
There is naught a statement with any self-sameness even
To name 'The Guardian is speaking.'

"We must conclude that the solution to the issue
Whether these words say something true or false
Is that they are false—and false in the same way as
'The present King of France is bald' is false.

"Neither the sentences nor the objects
The sentences attempt to name can be found.
Consider the performative, 'I hereby name me 'me.'
Who is naming? I am. Is this answer sound?

"Well, of course not, because again, we have an
Infinite regress of *false* and *true,*
So there is no statement 'I am'
That exists to assign *true.* Don't rue.

"So we eventually come to know
That as soon as we think just 'I am,'
We have to conclude, 'Therefore, I am not.'
This naming, therefore, is just a sham.

"So after thinking all of these things through,
We get ready to return to
Talking like 'normal' people.
So this is what we have to do.

"We assign True one i to the statement
'All statements we find in an *L* are false.'
We then state this in the meta-language,
Return to the object language, and waltz.

"Within the object languages, talking groups
Are simply ignoring all of this inconsistency,
Picking what they want to be true and false,
Constrained only by the cliffs that they think they need to see.

"And since from the meta-level no *L* statements ever appear as true,
'All statements in an *L* are false.'
And because of the explosive inconsistency, it is necessarily true that
'All statements in an *L* are false.'

At the meta-level, Tarski's Law does not apply,
Because the meta-language is so poor.
So we don't say much there, but that we are
Speaking Truth there we can be very sure.

"So, as
OBJECT LANGUAGE
SENTENCES ARE ONLY USEFUL
FOR HELPING US TO
Stop cliff-falling and to prevent other such painful happenings,
And as there is no rational standpoint from which we can
meaningfully say My and my friends' sufferings counts, but
No other suffering does, we should be using object languages to
STOP ALL SUFFERING.
"We could start by using our words
To develop universal, unbiased love;
Next learn how to help everyone;
And then we could say to everyone we meet:
We-ly suffering-fleeing.
We-ly happiness-seeking.
I-ly way-knowing.
You-ly me-follow.
But let's start by saying that *Philosophy*
Does not mean 'the love of wisdom;'
"PHILOSOPHY MEANS 'THE
WISDOM OF LOVE.'"

Fearing-{[possibly] [(you-ly thinking and
You-ly, this-poem-ly reading) and you-ly are bored]}-ly.
Subject-ly changing.

At this moment, Gus, in all his orange glory,
Opened the door and made his way
Skillfully to our table and sat down.
I said to him, "Would you please stay?"

He said, "I can only stay as
Long as the conditions are just right.
But what I plan to say to her,
I'm sorry, may bring to Ella great fright."

Ella said, "I figured all along that
Gus was quite real.
Now that I see he, a noumena, may have,
Better I feel."

Caesar then spoke to her and began by saying
She was totally blind as to what is real and what is not.
"Factuality that I do have, darling, all of the Buddha's say,
Has sameness to that of which all your new friends have got,

"But computer animation, quite fine, is included in the
Conditions from which I arise.
So let me talk to you of my interpretation of what you saw.
What I say will be a surprise.

"I suspect you felt sympathy for all of us simians,
But then you dismissed feeling sympathy as a source of obligation.
You probably to yourself, "Since these apes can reason,
We humans must, now, respect the dignity of the simian nation."

"But your source in the noumenal self
Of the rules all humans must follow
Is something that I must deny
As a thought that is simply hollow.

"Although we simians acquired
The ability to think with greater sophistication,
I deny that we can dismiss our sentient brothers.
Notice, we apes retained a failure of imagination.

"We simians saw ourselves as good—as probably you did, too—
And saw the humans, who didn't care for us, as inherently bad.
The ignorance we left behind changed our ability to know, but it
Remained profoundly deficient, because we didn't see them as sad.

"Another theme of this movie can be seen
If you know that it's part of a series,
Explaining why we go round and around the circle of woe.
True Ignorance causes all misery.

""It's quite clear to see, when you watch all the misery inflicted by
Humans upon the apes, some of the conditions that are in
The explanation of how the anger of the apes arose. Until
Both know the most important condition, neither side can win.

"What you told and accepted about animals
Being on earth just for humanity
Causes these species incalculable harm,
Truly showing your real insanity.

"All beings suffer from the same madness.
We see ourselves and other things apart.
We grasp both ourselves and what we want.
All the suffering in the world from this starts.

"So please don't think your self is real and
The one I have is not
So that you can stop clinging to the ignorance
That stops what joy we've got.

"The cruelty our minds inflict upon ourselves and others
Is really quite absurd.
Now that you've heard these words from me,
All that you need you've heard."

When Gus had spoken all he needed to say,
All eyes turned to Ella, who had resisted swallowing and was trying
To vomit the words that had fallen upon her ears.
None of us knew what to say.
Watching Ella, we were breathing deeply,
Almost gasping,
As we tenuously clung to the lives of our own confusions.

Suddenly, Ella burst into tears, and she began shaking uncontrollably.
Tears gushed down her cheeks.
Ten other eyes in our collection misted over with sadness.
I looked into the Mother's eyes and saw an ocean of compassion
Into which Ella's tears poured and mixed.
They were raindrops falling into and mixing with deep water.
We observers remained tenuously gathered into one aggregation,
As if straw-bound together only by twine spun
from the mist of our emotion,
And it was as if Ella had become the turbulent Niagara River
Rushing over its precipice.
We were the mist of that river.
River was falling into Earthquake, Earthquake was rising up to River,
And they poured into one another.

Then just as suddenly, Ella's tears dried up.
Her eyes became clear and azure blue, as if
She had awakened and become the cloudless sky of
a Colorado morning.
She was gazing with a firm grip on love.
The Child slowly lowered her eyes until they rested upon the Mother.
She calmly said in a hushed tone,
"You must become my Mother; now I want all of us to go home.
I've been schooled in the ways of the man who is the
Father of my future."
All of our eyes came to rest upon the Mother,
And no one would shift their gaze.
The straw dissolved into the twine that remained,
And then the twine was gone.

With Ella looking into that ocean of compassion,
The Mother held her in the all-enveloping arms of her love
As the Child to whom she was about to lay bare her breasts.
"Please tell me what you have learned about the Father."

"The Father cannot be separated from the Children.
This I thought could be done
And that we must cut free the Father from the slavery of our love
So we could see that
God and we legislate, both together and separately,
The rules of righteousness,
Needing only the concepts of freedom and legislation to do this.
But the Father cannot be separated, neither from Sons nor from Daughters.
The Father sees through the eyes of Daughters and Sons,
The Children see through the eyes of the Father,
And Children must learn to see through the eyes of the Mother.
Father and Mother, together, lead their Children home.
I am holding the hand of the Father.
Mother, please take all of us home."

With Ella's eyes now resting upon the Mother,
All things appeared to her to be dissolving
Into that vast ocean of compassion.
She was quite calm and blissfully gazing.
The Mother said, "Ella, you have become very still and quiet.
Tell the Mother about your Seeing."

"I am Seeing no things and everything, Mother.
Only what I am Seeing isn't sounding like Emptiness to me.
In Seeing, there are no things separate from me.
In Seeing, there is no separateness of me from things.
I am Seeing all things as if they were sweet water pouring into an Ocean of Compassion
And a sweet Ocean of Compassion pouring into water.
In Seeing in this way, I might name using *Emptiness.*
I might name using *Home, Ocean, God,* or *Allah.*
With
The *Goddess, Brahman,*
Or *G-D,*
I might name.
Using any holy name, I might name.
Should I name using *Emptiness* or may I use some other name I like, Mother?"

"You" may answer "Ella."
"I" may answer "Ella."
"We" may answer "Ella."
"They" may answer "Ella."
"Someone" may answer "Ella."
"No one" may answer "Ella."

In naming, there is nothing which can have its own true name.
In naming, all things are made, and all things are mere name.
In being named, there is nothing which can have its own true name.
In being named, all things are made, and all things are mere name.
So, "self-outside-of-naming" is neither naming nor being named,
But we ignorantly are grasping at these figments we have framed,
And this naiveté is causing everybody's pain.

!
"Then."
Mere "Child."
Merely named "Ella."
Merely, blissfully Peace-saying.

"For more information, please visit terrencemoore.us"

www.ingramcontent.com/pod-product-compliance
Ingram Content Group UK Ltd.
Pitfield, Milton Keynes, MK11 3LW, UK
UKHW041941190726
13854UKWH00004B/1716

9 781449 740917